YOSEMITE
THE COMPLETE GUIDE

5th Edition

©2018 DESTINATION PRESS & ITS LICENSORS
ISBN 13: 978-1-940754-29-1

Written & Photographed
by James Kaiser

This book would not have been possible without the help of many generous people. Special thanks to Beth Pratt, Kenny Karst, Pete Divine, Bob Fry, Greg Stock, Greg Cox, Linda Eade, Chris Stein, Paul Rogers, Jean Redle, Josia Lamberto-Egan, Maria Matijasevic, Peter Bohler, Peter Brewitt, Cat Zusky, Bob & Mary Anderson, the Yosemite Conservancy, the entire staff at YNP, and everyone who spent time with me in the wilderness. Above all, special thanks to superstar ranger Dick Ewart, whose wisdom and humor have inspired thousands of visitors, including me.

As always, a very special thanks to my family, friends, and all the wonderful people I encountered while working on this guide.

All information in this guide has been exhaustively researched, but names, phone numbers, and other details do change. If you encounter a change or mistake while using this guide, please send an email to changes@jameskaiser.com. Your input will help make future editions of this guide even better.

Additional Photography & Image Credits

Getty Images: 6; National Park Service: page 85, 86, 87, 88, 89, 95, 98, 102, 105, 106, 111, 113, 155; North Wind Picture Archives: 65, 90, 93, 96, 96, 103; Wildlife Stock Photos: 74–83; Peter Bohler: 21, 236
Printed in China

YOSEMITE

• THE COMPLETE GUIDE •

5th Edition

FSC
www.fsc.org

MIX
Paper from
responsible sources
FSC® C005748

JAMES KAISER

CONGRATULATIONS!

If you've purchased this book you're going to Yosemite. Perhaps you're already here. If so, you're in one of America's most extraordinary national parks—an alpine wonderland home to soaring cliffs, thundering waterfalls, and vast stretches of pristine, untouched wilderness. The Sierra Nevada Mountains are home to some of the most stunning natural scenery in North America, and Yosemite is, in my opinion, the crown jewel of the Sierra Nevada.

When I first started working on *Yosemite: The Complete Guide*, I figured it would take one year to complete. It took three. There was so much to photograph, so much that changed from season to season, that one year, I soon realized, could never do the park justice. As I hiked the trails and wandered the backcountry, I became friends with some of Yosemite's most legendary rangers, men and women who had spent decades in the park. Over long talks by the campfire they imparted their love and knowledge of Yosemite to me. It's my goal to pass that love and knowledge on to you.

Yosemite is amazing, but it can be an incredibly overwhelming place. You could easily spend a month here and not run out of things to do. But if you're like most people, you've only got a few days. Make those few days count! With a limited amount of time, you've got to plan your trip wisely. This book puts the best of Yosemite at your fingertips, helping you maximize your time for an unforgettable vacation. Whether you're here to hike, here to sight-see, or just here to relax and hang out, *Yosemite: The Complete Guide* is the only guide you'll need.

Now let me show you the best that Yosemite has to offer!

CONTENTS

YOSEMITE VALLEY P.123

The most famous part of the park, home to soaring cliffs, towering granite domes, and six waterfalls over 1,000 feet tall. Yosemite Valley is, without question, one of America's most beautiful places.

GLACIER POINT P.191

Perched on the edge of Yosemite Valley's south rim, Glacier Point offers sweeping panoramas 3,000 feet above the Valley floor. Sunsets are spectacular, and clear nights provide some of the best stargazing in California.

TIOGA ROAD P.221

This 46-mile road takes you deep into the heart of the High Sierra—a gorgeous alpine wilderness filled with shimmering lakes, snow-capped peaks, and some of the park's most amazing scenery.

TUOLUMNE MEADOWS P.247

Kick back in the Sierra Nevada's largest high altitude meadow and escape the summer crowds. Tuolumne Meadows is an oasis of tranquillity and the starting point for many of Yosemite's best hikes.

WAWONA & HETCH HETCHY P.295, P.301

Wawona is home to the Mariposa Grove of giant sequoias, the largest grove of big trees in the park. Hetch Hetchy—once a beautiful valley, now a flooded reservoir—set the stage for one of America's earliest environmental battles.

YOSEMITE TOP 5

TOP 5 VIEWPOINTS

TOP 5 ADVENTURES

TOP 5 HIKES

TOP 5 WATERFALLS

Vernal Fall

Half Dome Cables

INTRODUCTION

NESTLED DEEP IN the heart of California's Sierra Nevada Mountains, Yosemite is one of America's most spectacular national parks. Its alpine scenery is bursting with superlatives: the highest waterfall in North America (Yosemite Falls), the most famous vertical rock face in the world (El Capitan), and the largest organisms of all time (giant sequoias). But no statistic can ever capture the park's staggering beauty. Yosemite's sheer cliffs and thundering waterfalls have inspired some of America's finest artists, and its remarkable scenery continues to lure millions of visitors each year.

Yosemite Valley is the crown jewel of the park. Just seven miles long by one mile wide, it represents less than 1% of the park's 1,200 square miles. But concentrated among the Valley's forests, meadows, and 3,000-foot cliffs are some of the world's most remarkable natural features—Half Dome, El Capitan, Yosemite Falls. Because Yosemite Valley is the most popular part of the park, it's home to the vast majority of Yosemite's lodges, campgrounds and visitor facilities.

Above Yosemite Valley lies the High Sierra, a stunning alpine wilderness of shimmering lakes, snow-capped peaks, and oceans of sparkling granite. Reached via Tioga Road—the only east/west road that crosses the park—the High Sierra is an outdoor paradise for hikers, backpackers and rock climbers. Tuolumne Meadows, lying at an elevation of 8,600 feet, is the High Sierra's unofficial headquarters and the starting point for many spectacular hikes.

The park's southern tip is home to Wawona, famous for its proximity to the Mariposa Grove of giant sequoias (the largest of the park's three sequoia groves). Twenty miles north of Yosemite Valley lies Hetch Hetchy—once a beautiful valley, now a massive reservoir. Although its waterfalls are impressive in the spring, Hetch Hetchy is interesting mainly for the famous environmental battle it spawned nearly a century ago.

Yosemite Valley was first settled by the Ahwahneechee Indians. Following the Gold Rush, adventurous artists sought out the remote mountain valley, and their dramatic paintings and photographs made Yosemite famous. John Muir arrived in 1868, and his writings helped spur the creation of Yosemite National Park in 1890. In 1916 Ansel Adams made his first trip to the park, and starting in the 1930s rock climbers pioneered advanced techniques in Yosemite that are now used throughout the world. Today Yosemite's breathtaking cliffs, peaks and waterfalls lure over four million visitors a year.

Yosemite Valley

Half Dome, Winter

Above Red Devil Lake

HIKING &
BACKPACKING

THE SIERRA NEVADA mountains have some of the best hiking in North America, and Yosemite has some of the best hiking in the Sierra Nevada. Over 800 miles of trails crisscross Yosemite, ranging from easy day hikes to rugged multi-day backpacks. There are trails on the floor of Yosemite Valley, trails that skirt the Valley's rim, and trails that explore the High Sierra, the spectacular wilderness lying above 8,000 feet. Lush meadows? Glacial lakes? Thirteen thousand-foot peaks? Check, check and check. The only question is where not to hike.

Yosemite's hiking season gears up in the spring, when the Sierra Nevada's heavy winter snowpack starts to melt. As the months progress, the snow line creeps higher and higher, and by mid-July most of the park's trails are usually open. But conditions vary considerably from year to year. Following particularly heavy winters, Yosemite's highest trails can stay buried until late July. Always check current conditions before hitting the trail. Yosemite National Park's official website (nps.gov/yose) lists current trail conditions, but the staff at Yosemite's Wilderness Centers offer the ultimate insider tips.

Hiking in the spring and the early summer can be great—waterfalls and wildflowers abound!—but those months are also prime season for mosquitoes. Fortunately mosquito swarms are generally limited to the three weeks following snowmelt. But mosquito numbers, like snowfall, vary considerably from year to year. Some years they're bad, some years they're not. Ask about mosquito conditions if you visit in May, June or July, and always bring plenty of bug repellent.

July and August are the most popular hiking months. Other than the occasional afternoon thundershower, days are gloriously sunny and dry, and nights are clear under an ocean of stars. September is one of the best months for hiking—the crowds have thinned out and the days are sunny and mild—but temperatures at high elevations generally start plunging by the end of the month. The first big snowfall usually hits by mid-November, at which point Tioga Road and Tuolumne Meadows—the popular gateways to the High Sierra—shut down.

Day hikers can explore any trail whenever they like. Backpackers, however, must obtain permits to spend the night in the wilderness. Serious hikers and backpackers should also purchase a detailed topographic map. My personal favorite is National Geographic's *Trails Illustrated*, which shows day-use areas, campfire boundaries, and a wealth of other useful information.

Hiking Basics

- Carry and drink plenty of water
- Use strong UV protection
- Pets and bicycles are only allowed on paved trails
- Horses and mules have the right of way
- Pack out what you pack in

Wilderness Permits

Wilderness permits are required for all overnight backpacks in the park. Permits can be reserved in advance or picked up on the day of (or the day before) the start of your backpack at one of the park's five Wilderness Centers. Daily limits are placed on the number of permits issued for each trailhead About 60% of permits for a given trailhead can be reserved up to 24 weeks in advance. The remaining 40% are available up to 24 hours in advance on a first-come, first-served basis. The reservation system, while sometimes frustrating, was established to reduce over-crowding in the wilderness. By limiting the number of overnight hikers, the park ensures there are plenty of camping spots and a reasonable amount of solitude on the trail. Once you have a permit, it's great.

Permit reservation forms and trailhead availability are posted on the park's website (nps.gov/yose). When applying for a permit, you'll need the following information: entry trailhead, exit trailhead, dates of your trip, number of people in your party, and principal destination. Forms can be submitted by fax (209-372-0739) or mail (Wilderness Permits, PO Box 545, Yosemite, CA 95389). Reservations are also available by phone (209-372-0740). Permits cost $5 per reservation, plus $5 per person. If you plan to pick up a permit the day of—or better yet the day before—your backpack, arrive at the Wilderness Center as early as possible to beat the rush. During peak season in July and August, lines start forming at Wilderness Centers well before opening hours.

Wilderness Centers

There are five Wilderness Centers in Yosemite. Seasonal hours vary (check the *Yosemite Guide* or the park's website for exact hours of operation). A Wilderness Center at Badger Pass is also open in the winter.

- Yosemite Valley: located in Yosemite Village, next to the Ansel Adams Gallery
- Tuolumne Meadows: located just past the turnoff to Tuolumne Lodge
- Big Oak Flat Road: located next to the park's entrance station (Hwy 120)
- Wawona: located at Hill's Studio next to the Wawona Hotel
- Hetch Hetchy: located at the Hetch Hetchy Entrance Station

Weather Concerns

Summers in the Sierra Nevada are exceptionally sunny and dry, but anything can—and does—happen. In the summer, the biggest concern is afternoon thundershowers, which build with alarming speed when monsoonal systems occasionally pass over the mountains from the east. Do not attempt any exposed hike (Half Dome, Clouds Rest, etc.) if you see dark clouds in the sky. Thunderstorms typically develop between 2pm and 6pm. Follow this rule: up high by noon, down low by two. Also be aware that snow can fall at high elevations during any month of the year. Although snow is rare in the summer, it is possible, so be prepared. No matter when you hike, bring warm clothes and rain gear.

Guided Hikes & Backpacks

If you find Yosemite's vast network of trails a bit intimidating, or you're simply new to hiking or backpacking, consider spending some money on a guided hike. Two outstanding organizations offer guided hikes and overnight backpacks in the park, and many of the trips are led by Yosemite experts who point out fascinating plants, animals and geologic formations on the trail. The Yosemite Conservancy (yosemiteconservancy.org, 209-379-2317 x10) offers guided day hikes and overnight backpacks with an emphasis on outdoor education. Guided day hikes and overnight backpacks with tents, sleeping bags and other camping equipment provided are also available from Aramark (travelyosemite.com, 209-372-8344).

Backpacking Rules

WATER
Purify all drinking water using a giardia-rated filter, an iodine based chemical purifier, or by boiling 3–5 minutes.

CAMPFIRES
All campfires are prohibited above 9,600 feet. If you choose to build a campfire, use a previously impacted fire ring and use only dead and fallen wood.

CAMPSITES
Backcountry camping is prohibited within four miles of Yosemite Valley, Glacier Point, Tuolumne Meadows, Wawona and Hetch Hetchy. Backcountry camping is also prohibited within one mile of any road and within 100 feet of water. Whenever possible, campsites should be at least 100 feet from the trail.

FOOD STORAGE
Overnight hikers must store their food in bear canisters (see below). Metal bear boxes are provided at most trailheads for any food you choose to leave behind.

SOAP & TOOTHPASTE
Never use soaps (even "biodegradable" ones) or toothpaste in any lake, river, or stream. Use soap and toothpaste at least 100 feet away from any water source.

HUMAN WASTE
Backpackers must bury all human waste in a hole six inches deep at least 100 feet from water sources. Pack out all toilet paper.

Bear Canisters

Although generally harmless if undisturbed, black bears in Yosemite are notorious for attempting to raid backpackers' food. All wilderness visitors must take a bear canister to (a) protect their food and (b) prevent bears from becoming accustomed to human food.

For years backpackers were told to place their food in a bag, tie the bag to a rope, and hang the bag from a tall branch at night. At first, it worked. Then the bears started climbing onto the branches. These days the bag-and-rope system has been abandoned in favor of new, high-tech "bear canisters" that can hold up to a week's worth of food for one hiker. You can purchase bear canisters at outdoor stores throughout California or rent them from Yosemite's Wilderness Centers for $5. Lock all food and scented items (toothpaste, soap, etc.) in your bear canister and place it at least 30 feet from your tent at night. Before going to bed, double check that all food has been removed from your tent.

Yosemite's Best Hikes

The Mist Trail

Pohono Trail

Clouds Rest

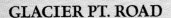

ROCK CLIMBING

TO SAY YOSEMITE is a good place to rock climb is like saying the Vatican is a good place to pray. To hardcore rock climbers, Yosemite is a holy mecca. Some of the world's most famous climbs are located in Yosemite Valley, and some of the sport's most innovative techniques and equipment were pioneered here. Today Yosemite's vast granite walls attract tens of thousands of climbers each year. Beginners come to learn, good climbers spend years becoming experts, and experts follow in the footsteps (and footholds) of climbing legends.

Rock climbing in Yosemite runs the gamut from easy bouldering (scampering over large boulders) to multi-day, 3,000-foot expeditions where climbers haul up food, water, and supplies, then spend the night strapped to a portable ledge. If a breezy night suspended thousands of feet in the air doesn't inspire your inner Spider Man, there are less intimidating ways to enjoy the sport. The Yosemite Mountaineering School offers rock climbing lessons in Yosemite Valley from mid-April through October (travelyosemite.com, 209-372-8344). Beginner, intermediate, and advanced lessons are offered, as well as two-day seminars on Big Wall Climbing. You can also hire private guides to lead you up Yosemite Valley's most storied landmarks, including El Capitan and Half Dome. They supply the equipment and food; you supply the cojones.

Summers are hot in Yosemite Valley (elevation: 4,000 feet), driving many rock climbers to the higher, cooler region around Tuolumne Meadows (elevation: 8,600 feet). In the summer, Yosemite Mountaineering School operates a sister branch in Tuolumne Meadows (209-372-8435) that also offers lessons.

A comprehensive guide to Yosemite rock climbing is beyond the scope of this book. If you're a bona fide rock jock, there are plenty of great climbing guides available in stores throughout the park.

Despite rock climbing's inherent danger, there are relatively few climbing accidents in Yosemite. The key word is relatively. There are still, on average, over 100 climbing accidents and 15 climbing parties that require rescue each year. When bad weather or injuries threaten climbers' lives, Yosemite Search And Rescue (YOSAR) steps into action. Their world-class team of superhuman climbers scampers up and down vertical walls in harrowing conditions, performing complex rescue operations thousands of feet above the ground. Their exploits are legendary, and their techniques are copied throughout the world.

For more on the history of rock climbing in Yosemite, see page 116.

Vogelsang

HIGH SIERRA CAMPS

YOSEMITE'S HIGH SIERRA Camps provide a fantastic way for visitors who enjoy a warm bed, a hot shower and a hearty meal in the beauty of the backcountry. There are five High Sierra Camps sprinkled throughout the park, each with a dining hall, shower house and several canvas tent cabins heated by wood burning stoves.

Each High Sierra Camp is located in a beautiful setting, and together they are connected by a 47-mile hiking loop. You can hike to any of the High Sierra Camps in a single day, or hike from camp to camp over several days, spending a night at each one. But due to the immense popularity of the High Sierra Camps, initial reservations are granted by a lottery in September and October for spots the following summer. You can enter the lottery by phone, mail or online (visit travelyosemite.com or call 801-559-4884 for details). If you miss the lottery or don't get a spot, additional dates become available in February on a first-come, first-served basis, and cancellations sometimes open up spots in the spring and summer. Rates at High Sierra Camps (including meals) are $161 per night for adults, $102 per night for children.

Another option is to pay for a multi-day Saddle Trip, riding from camp to camp on a mule, or a multi-day Guided Hike, led by a knowledgeable ranger who points out fascinating natural features as you hike from camp to camp. Saddle Trips and Guided Hikes are pricey ($1,115 for a 4-day Saddle Trip; $1,752 for a 6-day Saddle Trip; $928 for a 5-day Guided Hike; $1,442 for a 7-day Guided Hike), but they're definitely worth it (call 559-253-5672 for reservations).

The High Sierra Camps are generally open from early July to early September, but opening dates can be pushed back following winters with heavy snow. In 2005, a year which saw nearly 200% of average snowfall, the High Sierra Camps did not open at all.

What's the best High Sierra Camp? It's all a matter of taste. That said, Vogelsang, located at 10,300 feet, is consistently popular for its above-treeline views. And Glen Aulin, situated next to a gorgeous waterfall and reached by a stream-side trail, never fails to please.

Note: High Sierra Camp tent cabins are communal, which means your bed will be one of several in the tent cabin. Tent cabins are split male/female. Also note that Glen Aulin does not have showers.

HIGH SIERRA CAMPS

Glen Aulin p.262

May Lake p.234

Cathedral Lakes

Tenaya Lake

Porcupine Flat

Olmstead Point

Sunrise p.240

North Dome

Half Dome

Glacier Point

Merced Lake

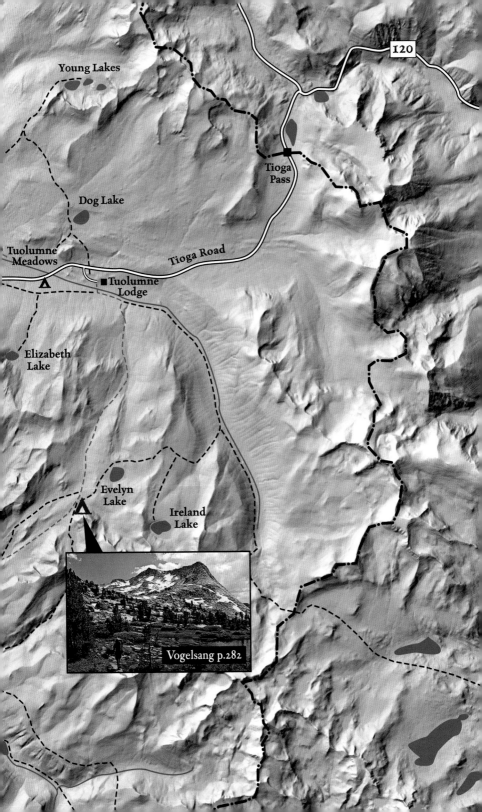

120

Young Lakes

Tioga Pass

Dog Lake

Tuolumne Meadows

Tioga Road

Tuolumne Lodge

Elizabeth Lake

Evelyn Lake

Ireland Lake

Vogelsang p.282

WINTER SPORTS

WHEN PEOPLE THINK Yosemite, they think glorious summer days filled with hiking, rock climbing, and plenty of mountain sunshine. But the Sierra Nevada—the second snowiest range in North America—is also a fantastic winter destination. And while ski resorts like Tahoe and Mammoth capture all the headlines, there's plenty of alpine fun to be had in Yosemite.

Badger Pass Ski Area (p.193) is located about 20 miles from Yosemite Valley along Glacier Point Road. It's hardly double diamond, but Badger Pass is a great beginner slope with reasonable prices and over 100 miles of cross-country ski trails. Several overnight cross-country ski trips are also offered. The most popular is the guided 10.5-mile ski trip from Badger Pass to Glacier Point, where you'll spend the night in a cozy hut on the rim of Yosemite Valley. Prices range from $350 for a one-night trip to $550 for a two-night trip, meals included. Guided six-day trips in the High Sierra are also offered ($876). All guided trips are offered by Aramark (209-372-8444, travelyosemite.com).

Another option is a self-guided overnight trip to Ostrander Ski Hut, located on Ostrander Lake (p.196), nine miles southeast of Badger Pass. This stone building offers 25 beds, cooking facilities and plenty of rustic charm—all for just $35 per night (yosemiteconservancy.org).

RIVER RAFTING

THE MERCED RIVER, which twists and turns through Yosemite Valley before exiting the park near the town of El Portal, offers two kinds of rafting experiences: mellow and exciting.

Mellow: Curry Village rents four-person rafts to paddle down the Merced River in Yosemite Valley. You'll pass spectacular views of Half Dome, Yosemite Falls and El Capitan as you float three gentle miles to Sentinel Beach, where a shuttle picks you up and takes you back to Curry Village. Raft rentals are available when the Merced is not flowing too high or too low—a window that generally lasts between late May and July. Cost: $31 per person.

Exciting: When the Merced River exits the park, it roars through dozens of rapids alongside Highway 140. A handful of rafting companies offer half-day and full-day trips in the spring and early summer. Cost: $110-170 per person. The best outfitters include OARS (800-346-6277, oars.com), Zephyr (800-431-3636, rafting.com), ARTA (800-323-2782, arta.org), and Whitewater Voyages (800-400-7238, whitewatervoyages.com). OARS and Zephyr also offer day and overnight trips on the even wilder (and in my opinion more scenic) Tuolumne River below Hetch Hetchy Reservoir. OARS even offers Tuolumne trips that combine rafting with gourmet food and wine/craft beer tastings at night!

Astronomy in Yosemite

Today nearly two-thirds of Americans live where they can no longer see the stars due to "light pollution" (manmade light). But here in Yosemite National Park, which boasts some of the darkest skies in California, the Milky Way still blazes across the sky. If you're not looking up at the stars, you're literally missing half the show. Don't know much about astronomy? Free ranger star talks are offered (check the park newspaper for dates and times), and every Saturday night in June, July and August local astronomy clubs set up telescopes on Glacier Point for public viewing.

Yosemite
BASICS

Getting to Yosemite

Yosemite National Park is located in the heart of California's Sierra Nevada Mountains. By car it's a roughly 4-hour drive east of San Francisco, a 6-hour drive northeast of Los Angeles, and a 3–hour drive south of Reno, Nevada. Amtrak (800-872-7245, amtrak.com) and Greyhound (800-231-2222, greyhound.com) offer service to the town of Merced, about 65 miles southwest of the park. From Merced you can purchase a ticket on YARTS (Yosemite Area Regional Transportation, 877-989-2787, yarts.com), which runs daily buses to Yosemite Valley from the towns of Merced, Mariposa, Midpines and El Portal along Highway 140. In the summer YARTS also offers service from Mammoth Lakes on the eastern side of the Sierra Nevada.

There are four entrances to Yosemite. Big Oak Flat Entrance, located on the park's western boundary along Highway 120, is the closest entrance to San Francisco. Arch Rock Entrance, located on Highway 140, is the closest entrance to the towns of Merced, Mariposa and Midpines. South Entrance is located along Highway 41 at the park's southern tip, close to Wawona and the Mariposa Grove of giant sequoias. Yosemite's only eastern entrance, Tioga Pass, is located at an elevation of 9,941 feet. Closed for much of the year due to heavy snow, Tioga Pass is accessible in the summer and early fall via Highway 120 from the small town of Lee Vining.

Entrance Fees

A seven-day pass to Yosemite National Park costs $30 per vehicle, $25 per motorcycle, or $15 per pedestrian or cyclist. An annual Yosemite pass costs $60. The best value, however, is the America The Beautiful Pass ($80), which gives you unlimited access to all U.S. national parks and federal recreation lands for one year (or a lifetime if you're 62 or older).

Getting Around Yosemite

The park operates a free shuttle in Yosemite Valley throughout the year. A free shuttle is also offered along Tioga Road between Tioga Pass and Olmstead Point in the summer. Seasonal shuttle times are listed in the *Yosemite Guide*.

Information

As soon as you enter the park, pick up a copy of the *Yosemite Guide*. This free park publication, available at all entrance stations and visitor centers, offers a wealth of seasonal information, including shuttle schedules, hours of operation for shops and restaurants, sunrise/sunset times and other park essentials.

Ranger-staffed visitor centers are located in Yosemite Valley (p.123), Tuolumne Meadows (p.247) and Wawona (p.297). Information booths are located in all park hotels.

Yosemite's Twitter feed, @YosemiteNPS, is a great resource for up-to-the-minute weather updates and park alerts.

Gas

One very important note on gas: **There are NO GAS STATIONS in Yosemite Valley.** There are only two gas stations in the park, located at Crane Flat and Wawona. Both have 24-hour pumps. Although relatively pricey, they are generally cheaper than gas stations just outside the park.

One Perfect Day in Yosemite

The late, great Yosemite ranger Carl Sharsmith was once asked what he would do if he only had one day in Yosemite. His response: "I'd go down to the Merced River, put my head in my hands, and cry."

Yes, you could spend months exploring Yosemite, but you can still have a great time in just one day. Head straight to Yosemite Valley (p.123) and bask in the park's most spectacular sights. Consider taking a narrated tram tour (p.125) in the morning, then pick up sandwiches at Degnan's Deli (p.126). Head to the Mist Trail (p.166), hike to the top of Vernal Fall, then find a nice spot for a picnic lunch. Finish your day with a drive to Glacier Point (p.196) for sunset and stargazing. (If the sunset crowds at Glacier Point are a bit much, hike to the top of nearby Sentinel Dome).

Another Perfect Day in Yosemite

After exploring the park highlights in Yosemite Valley, head to the stunning alpine wilderness above 8,000 feet known as the High Sierra. The adventure begins on Tioga Road (p.221). Along the way, be sure to visit the Tuolumne Grove of giant sequoias (p.224) and Olmstead Point (p.224), where you can check out the backside of Half Dome. If you're short on time, drive as far as Tenaya Lake (p.229). If you've got time to spare, head all the way to Tuolumne Meadows (p.247) and hike to the top of Lembert Dome (p.256).

When to Visit Yosemite

SPRING

Spring is the best time to visit Yosemite Valley. The waterfalls are at their peak, the wildflowers are blooming, and the summer crowds have not yet arrived. Daytime temperatures are often divine, but be prepared for chilly temperatures at night. In early spring, Tioga Road and Glacier Point Road are still closed due to lingering winter snow, restricting access to Tuolumne Meadows and Glacier Point. Both roads generally open by late May, but they can sometimes stay closed through June following winters with heavy snow.

SUMMER

Summer is Yosemite's most popular season in terms of visitation. The park's famously sunny weather draws a steady stream of vacationing families. (On average, just three percent of Yosemite's annual precipitation falls in the summer.) On many summer weekends, however, Yosemite Valley is a bit *too* popular, with long lines and traffic jams throughout the day. By mid-summer many of the Valley's famous waterfalls have run dry, and daytime temperatures often soar into the 90s. For all of these reasons, savvy Yosemite visitors head to Tuolumne Meadows in July and August. While Yosemite Valley (4,000 feet) is hot and crowded, Tuolumne Meadows (8,600 feet) is literally a breath of fresh air.

FALL

Fall is great time to visit Yosemite Valley. The crowds thin out dramatically after Labor Day, and daytime temperatures also start to cool down. September is one of the best months for hiking and rock climbing in Yosemite Valley. In Tuolumne Meadows, meanwhile, September brings crisp days and freezing nights. Services shut down on Tioga Road by the end of September, and the road closes after the first heavy snow (generally sometime between mid-October and mid-November). In Yosemite Valley, even the biggest waterfalls have slowed to a trickle by mid-October, but the autumn foliage is gorgeous.

WINTER

Winter is Yosemite's least popular season in terms of visitation, but after a fresh layer of snow the scenery is spectacular. Tioga Road is completely shut down in the winter, cutting off vehicle access to Tuolumne Meadows and the High Sierra. But Glacier Point Road is plowed as far as Badger Pass, a small ski resort with downhill and cross country skiing. Ranger-guided showshoe walks are also offered at Badger Pass. In Yosemite Valley, the Ahwahnee Hotel offers a number of great events, including wine tastings, Chefs' Holidays, and the famous Christmas Bracebridge Dinner. During the last two weeks of February, hundreds of visitors come to Yosemite Valley hoping to catch of glimpse of the Firefall (p.157), one of Yosemite's most amazing natural spectacles.

Black Bears

No other Yosemite topic generates as much fear and confusion as black bears (p.76). Grainy videos of bears breaking into cars are played on a constant loop on TV monitors in hotel lobbies, and overnight guests are required to sign forms stating they are "Bear Aware." Although bears can sometimes be problematic, you won't have to worry about them if you follow a few basic rules.

There are hundreds of hungry black bears in Yosemite, but they're not interested in you. They're interested in your food. Any food or scented items (toothpaste, sunscreen, etc.) left unattended or improperly stored serves as a bear magnet. As a result, proper food storage is required at all times. Anything with a scent (including canned goods, empty coolers, and dirty dishes) should be stored in metal food lockers, which are found throughout the park. Never leave any food or scented items in your tent or tent cabin. Never keep food in a hotel room with any doors or windows open. And never leave food in your car after daylight hours. If a bear sees or smells food in a car, it might break the windows and rip open the doors. Bears sometimes break into cars if they simply see a cooler—even if it's empty. Failure to store your food properly can also result in a federal fine of up to $5,000!

If you see a bear in a developed area (such as a campground) or if a bear approaches you, make as much loud noise as possible to scare it away. This is easier said than done, but yelling or banging on pots and pans is often enough to scare the bear away. Bear sightings should also be reported to park rangers.

Backpackers must also follow special food storage procedures (p.32). If you encounter a bear in the wilderness, maintain plenty of distance. This is especially important with cubs, because mamma bear might not be far behind.

Death In Yosemite

Most first-time Yosemite visitors worry about black bears and wild animals. But no one has ever been killed by a bear in Yosemite, and only one person (a small child) has ever died due to a rattlesnake bite. Horses, meanwhile, have been responsible for six deaths. Falling trees have killed nine people in the past 150 years, while rockfalls have killed 14.

Far more dangerous is suicide, which has claimed over 60 lives. Over 100 people have died while rock climbing, though most fatalities have occurred on descents rather than ascents. Over 140 people have died due to drowning, and over 40 people have been swept over waterfalls.

So what's the biggest killer in Yosemite? Motor vehicles, which have been responsible for over 160 deaths.

Yosemite Lodging & Camping

Yosemite's hotels are operated by Aramark Corporation (travelyosemite.com). Book your room as far in advance as possible, especially for the busy summer months. Note: When Aramark became the new Yosemite concessionaire in 2016, the previous concessionaire, Delaware North Corporation, asked for payment of $44 million for the use of "intangibles" including the historic names of hotels, which they had copyrighted. As of this writing, the case is still in court, but Aramark has changed the name of several historic hotels. Until this case is resolved, I've included both the new and historic names in this book.

Yosemite's 13 campgrounds are run by the National Park Service. Roughly half of the campgrounds are first-come, first-served; the rest require advance reservations (877-444-6777, recreation.gov). Campsites generally accommodate up to six people. There are also three Backpacker Campgrounds where backpackers with wilderness permits can spend the night before and after their trip without advance reservations. Yosemite's three Backpacker Campgrounds are located in Yosemite Valley, Tuolumne Meadows and Hetch Hetchy.

Lodging in Yosemite Valley

MAJESTIC YOSEMITE HOTEL / AHWAHNEE
This historic lodge (p.162) is the pinnacle of luxury in Yosemite. Rooms start at $460 per night and can go higher than $1,100 per night.

YOSEMITE VALLEY LODGE / YOSEMITE LODGE AT THE FALLS
The hotel rooms at Yosemite Valley Lodge can't compete with the luxury of the Majestic Yosemite Hotel/Ahwahnee, but the prices are far more reasonable. A few deluxe rooms have views of nearby Yosemite Falls (p.132).

HALF DOME VILLAGE / CURRY VILLAGE
This labyrinthine collection of canvas tent cabins offers the best budget lodging in Yosemite Valley. The simple tent cabins are charming, but the paper-thin walls can be a drag if you've got noisy neighbors. If you're looking for peace and quiet, book one of the wooden cabins, which are more expensive but nicer and more private. There is also a deluxe cabin with a working fireplace.

HOUSEKEEPING CAMP
Like Curry Village, Housekeeping Camp offers budget lodging. But while the canvas tent cabins at Curry Village feel rustic and charming, Housekeeping Camp's bunker-style shelters feel stark and bare. Still, nothing can take away from Housekeeping Camp's spectacular location along the banks of the Merced River. A few shelters even have terrific river views.

Camping in Yosemite Valley

There are four campgrounds in Yosemite Valley. The three "Pines" campgrounds, located at the eastern end of Yosemite Valley, all require reservations. Book campsites as far in advance as possible (877-444-6777, recreation.gov). Only Camp 4 is first-come, first-served, but long lines often form early in the morning for any available campsites. (Note: hot showers can be purchased at Half Dome/Curry Village and Housekeeping Camp in the afternoon.)

UPPER PINES CAMPGROUND
Open year-round, 238 sites, RVs up to 35 feet, $26/night.

LOWER PINES CAMPGROUND
Open April–October (approximately), 60 sites, RVs up to 40 feet, $26/night.

NORTH PINES CAMPGROUND
Open March–October (approximately), 81 sites, RVs up to 40 feet, $26/night.

CAMP 4
Camp 4 (p.136), located just east of Yosemite Falls, is the only first-come, first-served campground in Yosemite Valley. Open year-round, 35 sites, no RVs, $6 per person/night (a total of six people will be assigned to each campsite).

Lodging in Tuolumne Meadows

TUOLUMNE MEADOWS LODGE
Tuolumne Lodge offers 69 canvas tent cabins that are nearly identical to the tent cabins in Half Dome/Curry Village, but with the added bonus of a wood-burning stove to keep you warm at night. Bathrooms and hot showers are available at a central shower house. (888-413-8869, travelyosemite.com)

Camping in Tuolumne Meadows

There's only one campground in Tuolumne Meadows, but there are a handful of campgrounds between Yosemite Valley and Tuolumne Meadows along Tioga Road (see following page). There are also several small campgrounds located in Inyo National Forest just east of Tioga Pass. (Note: hot showers can be purchased at Tuolumne Lodge in the afternoon.)

TUOLUMNE MEADOWS CAMPGROUND
This is the largest campground in the park (304 sites). Half of the sites can be reserved in advance; half are first-come, first-served. Open July to late-September (weather permitting), RVs up to 35 feet, $26/night.

For comprehensive lodging and camping info visit jameskaiser.com

Other Lodging in the Park

WHITE WOLF LODGE
Located along Tioga Road, White Wolf Lodge consists of 24 canvas tent cabins with wood-burning stoves and four wooden cabins with propane heat.

BIG TREES LODGE / WAWONA HOTEL
This large, historic hotel (p.297) is bursting with Victorian charm. Some rooms have private baths, others do not. Located in Wawona near the park's southern boundary.

Other Campgrounds in the Park

BRIDALVEIL CREEK CAMPGROUND
Located about halfway up Glacier Point Road. Open July–September (weather permitting). First-come, first-served. 110 sites, $18/night, RVs up to 35 feet.

CRANE FLAT CAMPGROUND
Located near the junction of Big Oak Flat Road and Tioga Road. Open July to mid-October (weather permitting). Reservations available. 166 sites, $26/night, RVs up to 35 feet.

HODGDON MEADOW CAMPGROUND
Located near Yosemite's Big Oak Flat Entrance. Open year-round. Reservations required mid-April to mid-October. 105 sites, $26/night, RVs up to 35 feet.

TAMARACK FLAT CAMPGROUND
Located off Tioga Road, not too far from Crane Flat. Open late June–September (approximately). First-come, first-served. 52 sites, $12/night, no RVs.

WHITE WOLF CAMPGROUND
Located next to White Wolf Lodge off Tioga Road. Open July to mid-September (weather permitting). First-come, first-served. 74 sites, $18/night, RVs up to 27 feet.

YOSEMITE CREEK CAMPGROUND
Located off Tioga Road. Open July–early September (approximately). First-come, first-served. 40 sites, $12/night, no RVs.

PORCUPINE FLAT CAMPGROUND
Located along Tioga Road. Open July–mid-October (approximately). First-come, first-served. 52 sites, $12/night, RVs up to 24 feet.

WAWONA CAMPGROUND
Located in Wawona. Open year-round. Reservations required mid-May to mid-October. 93 sites, $26/night, RVs up to 35 feet.

Lodging & Camping near Yosemite

There are dozens of hotels and campgrounds outside the park, and listing them all would take dozens of pages. Rather than waste all that paper, I've posted comprehensive hotel and campground information at jameskaiser.com

Gateway Towns

MARIPOSA, MIDPINES & EL PORTAL

These three towns, located west of Yosemite's Arch Rock Entrance along Highway 140, are the closest gateway towns to Yosemite Valley. Mariposa, located about 30 miles (45-minute drive) from Arch Rock Entrance Station, is a small Gold Rush-era town. Its boardwalk-lined Main Street is filled with boutiques, restaurants and tap rooms. Mariposa is your best bet for dining outside the park, and if you don't mind the drive there are plenty of reasonably priced hotels. The tiny towns of Midpines and El Portal consist of a few scattered hotels and restaurants along Highway 140. If you're planning on spending most of your time in Yosemite Valley, but all hotels in Yosemite Valley are booked, look for lodging in one of these towns.

GROVELAND

Groveland, located along Highway 120 about 24 miles west of the park's Big Oak Flat Entrance, is another Gold Rush-era town. Its most famous institution, the Iron Door Saloon, is the oldest continually operating saloon in California, serving cold drinks and good food, plus live entertainment on the weekends. Groveland also has a handful of charming B&Bs.

FISH CAMP & OAKHURST

Just outside the park's southern entrance lies the tiny town of Fish Camp, which is home to a small general store and a handful of B&Bs. Fourteen miles south of Fish Camp is Oakhurst, Yosemite's largest gateway town. Downtown Oakhurst is filled with mini-malls and fast food restaurants. Like Mariposa, Oakhurst is a good bet for reasonably priced lodging if you don't mind the drive.

LEE VINING

The tiny town of Lee Vining, located at the eastern base of the Sierra Nevada Mountains, revolves almost entirely around Yosemite and Mono Lake tourism. If you're planning on spending the bulk of your time in Tuolumne Meadows and all nearby hotels are booked, look for lodging in Lee Vining. Note: Tioga Road, which bisects the park and connects Lee Vining to Tuolumne Meadows and Yosemite Valley, closes in the winter due to heavy snow.

For comprehensive lodging and camping info visit jameskaiser.com

GEOLOGY

Yosemite is a dazzling landscape that captivates everyone who sets foot in the park. Stretching from the western foothills to the jagged peaks on the Sierra's crest, Yosemite encompasses some of the most dramatic alpine scenery in America.

Even if you know nothing about geology, Yosemite is still an impressive sight. But take the time to learn about the forces that created it, and you'll look upon the park with a fresh set of eyes. What was once amazing will become astounding. What once took your breath away will make your head spin.

On a human timescale, Yosemite seems peaceful and serene. On a geological timescale, however, it is violent and exciting. The last glaciers to sweep through the park melted 10,000 years ago. In geological terms, 10,000 years is the blink of an eye. If the age of the Earth (4.5 billion years) was represented by a 24-hour clock, the past 10,000 years would only represent a fraction of the final second before midnight.

The glaciers sculpted graceful valleys, gouged out sheer cliffs, and polished the granite to a shine. They also bulldozed soil and vegetation out of the mountains, scraping the surface clean and creating a frozen landscape nearly devoid of life. The most recent glacial advance started around 50,000 years ago, but at least three distinct periods of glacial advance—and possibly 10 or more—have swept over the Sierra Nevada since the Ice Age began roughly 2.4 million years ago. Each glaciation added a new layer of depth and complexity to Yosemite's landscape, leaving behind thousands of dazzling new features. Today few places in the world offer so many textbook-perfect examples of glacial geology.

Prior to the Ice Age, tectonic forces had thrust up a massive, 400-mile long block of granite that created the Sierra Nevada. As the mountains rose up, ancient rivers raced down their slopes, carving out deep valleys that, in places, exceed the Grand Canyon in depth. By the time the Ice Age set in, the Sierra Nevada was already a fascinating landscape. Glaciers, it turns out, were simply the icing on an already remarkable cake.

ANCIENT ROCKS

YOSEMITE'S STORY BEGAN roughly 500 million years ago when North America lay near the equator and California lay under a warm tropical sea. As rivers flowed into the sea from North America, they flushed massive amounts of sediment offshore. Over time, as the layers of sediment grew thousands of feet thick, the bottom-most layers were compressed into sedimentary rocks. Then, as tectonic plates shifted and North America rotated and moved north—a process that took hundreds of millions of years—the sedimentary rocks were pushed up to form the ancient surface of California.

Around 210 million years ago, North America collided with a vast tectonic plate called the Farallon Plate, which lay under the ocean to the west. As the North American Plate overrode the Farallon Plate—a process geologists call subduction—the Farallon Plate was pushed several miles beneath North America, where extreme heat and pressure melted its leading edge. Vast pools of magma rose up under California, some of which reached the surface to form volcanoes. But most of the magma simply cooled into granite several miles below ground.

For the next 130 million years, as subduction of the Farallon Plate continued, enormous quantities of magma rose up under California in giant plumes called plutons. The plutons arrived in a series of pulses that lasted between 10 and 15 million years. By about 80 million years ago, the combined plutons formed a giant, underground mass of granite called a batholith (from the Greek words *bathos*, "deep," and *lithos*, "rock"). Throughout the formation of the Sierra Nevada Batholith, intense temperatures and pressures cooked the overlying sedimentary rocks, altering their chemical composition. Over time the sedimentary rocks were transformed (metamorphosed) into metamorphic rocks.

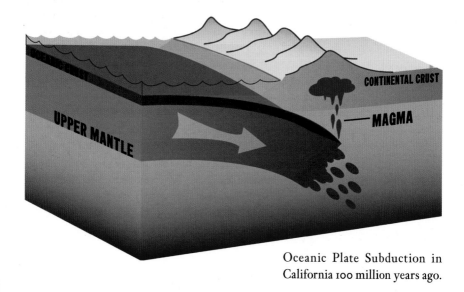

Oceanic Plate Subduction in California 100 million years ago.

THE MOUNTAINS RISE

AS SUBDUCTION SENT massive pools of magma rising under California, a chain of active volcanoes formed on the surface that, at their peak, may have towered as high as 18,000 feet above the landscape. But around 80 million years ago the magma stopped rising and the volcanoes became inactive. For the next 40 million years, erosion slowly ground down the mountains, removing the overlying metamorphic rock and exposing the underlying granite.

As the mountains rose up, the gradients of rivers increased, speeding their flow and accelerating their erosive power. The rivers carved deep canyons and flushed millions of tons of sediment into California's Central Valley, which lies just west of the Sierra Nevada. (Drive across the Central Valley today and you are driving across eroded Sierra Nevada sediments reaching depths of tens of thousands of feet.)

Around 20 million years ago, the western edge of North America came into contact with an entirely new tectonic plate: the Pacific Plate, which underlies much of the Pacific Ocean. But the collision between the Pacific Plate and the North American Plate was not head-on. Rather, the plates moved laterally in opposite directions, grinding against each other along their boundary and forming the San Andreas Fault.

As the two tectonic plates scraped against each other along the San Andreas Fault, huge pressures built up among interlocking rocks. Ultimately the rocks buckled, relieving pressure and jolting the land and causing earthquakes. But not all of the built-up pressure was concentrated on the San Andreas Fault. The force of the grinding plates fanned out across California, cracking the land and forming new, smaller faults.

As a complex set of pressures exerted themselves from multiple directions, a fault system formed near the eastern edge of the Sierra Nevada Batholith. The land rose up as if on a pivot from the west, creating a sheer eastern slope and a long, gentle western slope. Uplift started slowly around 10 million years ago, then accelerated several million years later. Before long, the modern Sierra Nevada towered 14,000 feet above the landscape.

Throughout the uplift of the Sierra Nevada, millions of cracks formed in the mountains' granite. Initial cracks formed due to pressures associated with uplift, followed by cracks that formed as erosion stripped away miles of overlying rocks, causing the underlying rocks to expand and crack. These cracks (called joints) are still forming today. Extending in every direction, they create a giant template for future erosion. Some cracks are vertical, some are horizontal, and some form in rounded concentric layers. The concentric cracks are the most fascinating, for they erode in curved sheets, flaking off like layers of an onion and leaving behind rounded domes (a process called *exfoliation*).

ICE AGE GLACIERS

AROUND 2.4 MILLION years ago, Earth entered the Ice Age. As global temperatures cooled and snowfall increased, a thick snowpack accumulated in the Sierra Nevada that, over time, compacted into massive sheets of ice. When the ice sheets were set into motion under the pressure of their own weight, they became glaciers. Pushing downhill, the glaciers consumed everything in their path. Boulders, soil, trees—everything but the bedrock was picked up and carried along. But even the bedrock did not escape unscathed. The glaciers—essentially dirty ice full of debris—acted like giant sheets of sandpaper, grinding down the bedrock and smoothing it out.

Then, abruptly, temperatures warmed and the glaciers retreated. Then they advanced and retreated again. And again. And again. Over the past 2.4 million years, as global temperatures have fluctuated, glaciers have advanced and retreated at least three times in the Sierra Nevada. At higher latitudes glaciers have advanced and retreated over a dozen times, and many geologists believe that Sierra Nevada glaciers followed a similar pattern. But because the Sierra Nevada glaciers erased everything in their path, including the evidence of previous glaciers, supporting facts are scarce.

The oldest and largest glacial advance in the Sierra Nevada, known as the pre-Tahoe glaciation, occurred roughly one million years ago. As pre-Tahoe glaciers descended from high elevations, they blanketed the mountains under a massive sheet of ice roughly 270 miles long by 40 miles wide. Only the highest peaks in the Sierra remained exposed, poking out like rocky islands in a sea of ice. All told, over half of Yosemite was covered by ice. Tuolumne Meadows was buried under 2,000 feet of ice, and Yosemite Valley was filled to the brim.

The force of the glaciers was massive. Under the largest glaciers, pressures topped several hundred pounds per square inch. Where the bedrock was weakened by cracks, glaciers plucked out large chunks of rock and carried them down to lower elevations. Where the bedrock was solid and relatively free of cracks, glaciers smoothed out the rock and formed glacial polish—a glassy veneer with a texture as smooth as polished marble. In places the glacial polish was scraped by rocks embedded at the bottom of the glacier, leaving behind distinct scratches called glacial striations.

Descending from high elevations—at speeds ranging from several inches to several feet per day—the glaciers flowed through previously formed river valleys that, cut by pre-Ice Age rivers, had steep V-shaped profiles. As the glaciers advanced through the V-shaped valleys, they gouged out the sides, leaving rounded U-shaped valleys in their wake.

As glaciers flowed down the mountains, picking up bits and pieces of the landscape along the way, the front of the ice bulldozed accumulated debris. When the ice reached lower, warmer elevations, the front of the glacier melted and

deposited the debris. Ice continued to flow from above, however, forming a kind of conveyor belt that transported even more loose material to the melting front of the glacier. These debris piles are called terminal moraines, and they mark the farthest extent of the glacier. A similar feature, called lateral moraines, formed along the sides of the glacier. Today many remnant terminal and lateral moraines mark the maximum extent of the glaciers that deposited them.

During each of the Sierra Nevada glaciations, glaciers advanced for tens of thousands of years. But as global temperatures warmed, the glaciers melted in a fraction of that time, and large boulders embedded in the ice settled on the underlying bedrock. These rocks, often carried miles from their points of origin, are called glacial erratics. Today they are found throughout the High Sierra.

At the end of the most recent glaciation—the Tioga glaciation, which ended roughly 10,000 years ago—temperatures warmed and the glaciers started to melt. By about 8,000 years ago, glaciers had completely disappeared from the Sierra Nevada. Since then, however, fluctuations in climate have triggered at least two additional periods of glacial advance and retreat (albeit on a much smaller scale). The most recent glaciation occurred from 1600 to 1850, when temperatures dropped during a period of global cooling called the Little Ice Age. During this time, roughly 100 small glaciers formed in the Sierra Nevada. But over the past 150 years, as global temperatures have risen, many of those glaciers have melted. Today only a handful of small glaciers remain in the Yosemite region.

Glacial Landscapes

As massive glaciers advanced over the High Sierra during the last Ice Age, they rounded and smoothed the underlying granite. Even today, the graceful glacially sculpted landscapes are clearly visible throughout Yosemite's high elevations.

Nunataks

At the height of the Ice Age one million years ago, only Yosemite's tallest peaks remained above the glaciers, poking out like rocky islands in a sea of ice. Although the glaciers rounded and smoothed the lower slopes of these mountains, their summits remained jagged and rough. Today these angular peaks, called nunataks, can be seen throughout the High Sierra.

GEOLOGY TODAY

GLACIERS PUT THE finishing touches on the Sierra Nevada, but erosion continues to chip away at the range. One of the most common acts of erosion is frost wedging, which occurs when water freezes and expands in the cracks of rocks, wedging and breaking them apart. Frost wedging is most active in the spring and fall when daily temperature fluctuations are greatest.

Earthquakes are also common in the Sierra Nevada, which is riddled with active faults along its eastern boundary. In 1872 an earthquake shook the ground near Lone Pine, California, which lies at the base of the eastern Sierra. The earthquake, which was probably bigger than the San Francisco earthquake of 1906, killed 27 people and pulverized nearly every building in town. In an instant, the mountains above Lone Pine jumped 13 feet higher and shifted 20 feet laterally. In Yosemite Valley, the early morning earthquake woke up John Muir, who stumbled outside to watch a lofty rock pinnacle crash to the ground. An observer near Nevada Falls claimed the waterfall stopped flowing for at least half a minute, and several thousand tons of rock shook free from nearby Liberty Cap, creating a powerful air blast that knocked a nearby building off of its foundation.

Earthquakes and other forms of erosion can also trigger rockfalls, which volume-wise are probably the most substantial form of erosion acting on Yosemite right now. Sometime around 1740 a massive rockfall took out 5.6 *million tons* of Slide Mountain (later named for the rock slide) in a remote, northern section of the park. Dozens of smaller rockfalls have taken place since, including a 2006 whopper along the Merced River Canyon west of Yosemite Valley. That rockfall buried 600 feet of Highway 140 and closed the road for nearly two months. As the years progress, erosion will chip away at the rockfall, reducing boulders to talus, talus to scree, scree to gravel, and gravel to sand.

Parts of the eastern Sierra Nevada are also volcanically active. Mammoth Mountain, home to the popular ski resort southeast of Yosemite, is a volcano that formed 400,000 years ago. And a large magma chamber exists under Mono Basin directly east of Yosemite. The last known volcanic event in the region was a mild underwater eruption at the bottom of Mono Lake in 1890. When, or where, the next eruption will occur is unknown.

Moving forward, the forces of geology will continue to reshape the landscape. Over hundreds of years, rockfalls will continue to erode Yosemite's cliffs. Over tens of thousands of years, vast glaciers could cover the mountains again if past cycles repeat themselves. And over millions of years, the park's most stunning features—Half Dome, El Capitan, Yosemite Falls—will disappear entirely. So consider yourself lucky. You're alive for that brief moment (geologically speaking) when Yosemite is filled with world-class scenery that generations of visitors have come to know and love.

Muir v. Whitney

The Formation of Yosemite Valley

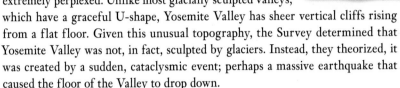

JOHN MUIR

When members of the California State Geologic Survey first studied Yosemite Valley in the 1860s, they grew extremely perplexed. Unlike most glacially sculpted valleys, which have a graceful U-shape, Yosemite Valley has sheer vertical cliffs rising from a flat floor. Given this unusual topography, the Survey determined that Yosemite Valley was not, in fact, sculpted by glaciers. Instead, they theorized, it was created by a sudden, cataclysmic event; perhaps a massive earthquake that caused the floor of the Valley to drop down.

Nature writer John Muir vehemently disagreed with the Survey's cataclysmic "drop down" theory. Having studied the effects of glaciers during his wanderings in the High Sierra, Muir was convinced that Yosemite Valley was indeed sculpted by glaciers. Although Muir had studied geology during his last two years at the University of Wisconsin, he was a scientific amateur, and members of the Geologic Survey laughed off his theory. Josiah Whitney, the Yale-educated head of the Survey, insisted there was no evidence to indicate that glaciers had ever occupied Yosemite Valley.

But Muir was confident in his beliefs, and the more he lectured on his theory, the more people listened. Finally, in 1870, Muir's theory was officially endorsed by the famous geologist Louis Agassiz and his student Dr. Joseph Le Conte, a professor at the University of California. Members of the State Geologic Survey were appalled. They hurled insults at Muir, calling him an "ignoramus" and "a mere sheepherder." Whitney stated that the glacier theory was "based on entire ignorance of the whole subject, [and] may be dropped without wasting any more time upon it."

In fact, the debate raged on for nearly 60 years. Then, in 1930, long after the deaths of both Whitney and Muir, the distinguished French geologist François Matthes announced that he agreed with Muir's theory, and the matter was laid to rest. In hindsight, Muir's theory was not entirely correct, even though it was extremely close. And while Whitney was wrong about the formation of Yosemite Valley, he did correctly identify Hetch Hetchy as a glacially sculpted valley. Regardless, the heated debate between Whitney and Muir became one of the classic amateur-beats-the-pro tales of geology.

JOSIAH WHITNEY

Rockfalls in Yosemite

Ever since glaciers departed roughly 15,000 years ago, rockfalls have been the main geologic force sculpting Yosemite. On average, there is a rockfall every 10 days in Yosemite Valley. And while the vast majority of them are small and insignificant, large rockfalls occasionally prove catastrophic.

One of the most famous rockfalls occurred in 1996 at the eastern end of Yosemite Valley. High above Happy Isles, two rocks totaling 40,000 cubic yards in size detached from the cliffs above. The rocks hit the ground traveling at 270 miles per hour, and the resulting wind blast exceeded 250 miles per hour. Over 700 trees toppled over like matchsticks. Remarkably, only one hiker was killed. (All told, 15 people have died due to rockfalls in Yosemite). The largest historic rockfall occurred in 1987, when roughly 800,000 cubic yards of debris tumbled down from the Three Brothers, closing Northside Drive for months.

But even these rockfalls pale in comparison to the extra-large rockfalls called rock avalanches. Although no rock avalanches have occurred in Yosemite Valley in recorded history, evidence of their past destruction abounds. Roughly 3,600 years ago, 3.75 million cubic yards of rock fell 2,500 feet down the eastern face of El Capitan. The resulting debris pile spread 2,200 feet past El Capitan's base. The largest known rock avalanche happened in Tenaya Canyon, when *15 million* cubic yards of rock came tumbling down the cliffs across from Half Dome. The resulting debris pile, 100 feet deep in places, dammed Tenaya Creek and created Mirror Lake.

Interestingly, there are relatively few rockfalls along Yosemite Valley's lower cliffs. This is because Ice Age glaciers, which never reached the rim during the last glaciation, scraped away many loose rocks from the lower cliffs. As a result, most rockfalls in Yosemite Valley initiate from the upper reaches of the cliffs, giving them a great deal of destructive energy.

Although relatively common, rockfalls are still shrouded in mystery. Geologists know that rockfalls can be triggered by earthquakes, the expansion of freezing water in cracks, and other erosive processes. But the trigger of many rockfalls is hard to determine. In a park as popular as Yosemite, the ability to understand and predict rockfalls could save many lives, but rockfall prediction—like earthquake prediction—has proven quite challenging.

Rockfalls have historically been difficult to study, but new technologies are starting to reveal their secrets. Geologists recently began using high resolution photography and LIDAR (terrain mapping with lasers) to make high resolution 3D maps of Yosemite's cliffs. By cross-referencing data from year to year, computers can determine where small sections of cliffs are missing, and therefore where previously unreported rockfalls have occurred. And as more and more visitors bring video cameras to Yosemite, more and more rockfalls are being captured on video, allowing geologists to better study their effects.

Slide Mountain

GREAT BASIN DESERT

SIERRA NEVADA

Lake
Tahoe

Yosemite
National
Park

Mono
Lake

SIERRA NEVADA

GREAT CENTRAL VALLEY

Pacific Ocean

Sierra Nevada Mountains

Running half the length of California, the Sierra Nevada is the longest, highest, and grandest mountain range in America. Although the Rockies and Appalachians are longer, they are technically mountain systems made up of several smaller ranges. The Sierra Nevada, by contrast, is a single unbroken range that is nearly as large as the French, Swiss, and Italian Alps combined. At roughly 26,000 square miles, it covers 17% of California.

From Fredonyer Pass in the north to Tehachapi Pass in the south, the Sierra Nevada stretches 420 miles, varying in width from 50 to 80 miles. The mountains are essentially a massive block of granite lifted like a trap-door on a western hinge. The long western slope rises gradually at a tilt of just 2 to 6 degrees, while the steep eastern slope plummets 25 degrees—dropping over two vertical miles in places.

Sierra peaks increase in elevation from north to south, reaching 10,000 feet near Lake Tahoe, 13,000 feet in Yosemite, and 14,000 feet near Mt. Whitney. At 14,495 feet, Mt. Whitney is the tallest peak in the continental United States. All told, the entire range contains roughly 500 peaks above 12,000 feet. Over half of the alpine Sierra (the area located above treeline) is exposed rock, and nearly all of it is protected as national parks or federally designated wilderness.

The Sierra is bounded in the west by California's Central Valley, where flat agricultural lands grow one quarter of America's food. As coastal air flows over the Sierra from the west, moisture is wrung out of the air as it rises and cools. Stripped of its moisture, the dry air heads east over Nevada and Utah, creating the Great Basin Desert.

Sierra summers are generally dry, but winters can dump up to 70 feet of snow. The heaviest snowfall occurs in the Central Sierra, which bears the brunt of winter storms that creep through San Francisco's Golden Gate—the most prominent gap in California's coastal mountains. In the spring, a combination of rain and snowmelt brings heavy runoff to the Sierra Nevada, but by autumn many streams have slowed to a trickle.

Only a handful of rivers tumble down the Sierra's steep eastern flank. Flowing into the Great Basin Desert, their waters never reach the sea. On the gentle western slope, 11 major rivers flow into the Central Valley, eight of which join the Sacramento and San Joaquin rivers on their journey to San Francisco Bay. Many western Sierra rivers have cut dramatic valleys thousands of feet deep. The largest, Kings Canyon, is deeper than Grand Canyon, with walls over 7,000 feet high.

Lyell Glacier

Resting on the northern slope of Mt. Lyell (the highest peak in the park), Lyell Glacier is the largest glacier in Yosemite. It's also the second largest glacier in the Sierra Nevada and one of the southernmost glaciers in North America. Both the mountain and the glacier are named for Charles Lyell, whose 1830 book *Principles of Geology* has been called "the most seminal work in geology." (Ironically, when the theory of Ice Ages was first advanced in the 1830s, Lyell did not believe it, and he argued against it for decades.) Over the past century, Lyell Glacier has been shrinking due to warming temperatures. In 2013 it was determined that Lyell Glacier is no longer moving, and thus should be technically classified as an "ice field."

Lyell Glacier, 2006

ECOLOGY

COVERING 1,200 SQUARE miles and over 10,000 feet of mountainous elevation, Yosemite is home to thousands of fascinating plants and animals. Giant sequoias, the largest organisms on the planet, have been living at the park's mid elevations for thousands of years, while delicate alpine flowers measure their lives in weeks among the park's highest peaks. The forests in between are home to black bears, mountain lions, bobcats, deer, and dozens of smaller animals. All told, over 80 species of mammals, over 150 species of birds, and over 1,400 species of plants have been identified in the park.

Plants and animals live only where factors such as temperature, sunlight, and access to food and water favor their survival. Because plants form the foundation of a thriving food chain, ecologists have divided the Sierra Nevada into half a dozen vegetative zones—five of which occur in Yosemite. These zones, based loosely on elevation, provide an easy way to visualize a complex system. Boundaries between zones are often fuzzy, with some species living in two or three zones and with many microclimates within each zone. But such complexity is to be expected in a place where the landscape changes so fast. Driving from the arid plains of the Great Central Valley to Tioga Pass—at 9,943 feet the highest paved road in California—is the ecological equivalent of driving from Mexico to Alaska in a single day.

Taken as a whole, the Sierra Nevada boasts many impressive statistics. It's the highest unbroken mountain range in the continental U.S. and the second snowiest range on the continent (after the Cascades in the Pacific Northwest). Over 3,500 plant species are found in the Sierra Nevada—a number greater than the total number plant species found in the entire state of Florida. And the Sierra Nevada's alpine region, which lies above treeline, has the largest, richest flora of any alpine area in North America. All told, it's home to nearly 200 species found nowhere else in the world. But like environments everywhere, the Sierra Nevada is constantly changing. Geological forces, fluctuating climate, and human influences that started with the arrival of Indians have all shaped the present environment—and will continue to shape it in the years to come. How the modern distribution of plants and animals came to be, and how it operates today, is one of the most fascinating aspects of Yosemite.

A CHANGING LANDSCAPE

YOSEMITE'S MODERN ECOLOGY started to take shape around 15,000 years ago when Ice Age glaciers started to melt. The glaciers had scraped away soil and vegetation, and when the ice melted it revealed a barren landscape filled with expanses of smooth, glistening granite. The scenery back then must have been extraordinary—hundreds of square miles of bare granite billowing down from the highest peaks. Bedrock depressions scooped out by the glaciers filled with meltwater, creating thousands of new lakes, but much of the landscape was essentially lifeless.

The formation of soil, a combination of disintegrated rock and decomposed organic material, was an extremely slow process. Granite is one of the most erosion-resistant rocks on the planet, and organic material in the wake of the glaciers was sparse. But over thousands of years, after lichens and other hardy colonizers had gained a foothold, a thin layer of topsoil built up, making the mountains habitable for progressively larger plants. Eventually, enough topsoil built up to support sun-loving trees, which thrived in the open, sunny landscape. When a shady forest canopy developed, shade-loving trees also took root.

Ecologists call this ongoing process of new plant arrival in response to changing conditions *succession*. In the long term, succession occurs as fluctuating climate alters temperature and precipitation, which changes the composition of forests and meadows. In the short term, succession occurs when forests are disturbed by fire, avalanches, or insect infestations. As the composition of the forest changes, so do the species of plants and animals living there. Some species thrive in sunny open spaces, while others prefer mature forests.

Over the past 10,000 years, as environmental conditions have changed, Sierra Nevada's ecology has changed with them. Temperatures have warmed considerably since the melting of the glaciers, but the rate of warming has not been steady. As temperatures fluctuated, Sierra Nevada vegetation marched up and down the mountains accordingly, shifting to higher elevations during periods of warming and retreating to lower elevations during periods of cooling. Changing climate also affects precipitation. The past 1,200 years have seen two major droughts, each lasting 100 to 200 years, while the past 150 years have been relatively warm and wet, containing one of the wettest half centuries of the past 1,000 years. All of this, combined with modern human influences, has affected forest density and wildfire patterns, laying the groundwork for the present forest composition.

Area-wise the Sierra Nevada covers just 20 percent of California, but the mountains contain over half of California's 7,000 plant species. Roughly one-third of Sierra plant species are endemic (found nowhere else in the world).

ECOLOGY TODAY

WINTERS IN THE Sierra Nevada bring massive amounts of snow—up to 50 feet in some places—with over 95 percent of the Sierra's annual precipitation falling between October and April. Summers, by contrast, are hot and dry, resulting in less than five percent of the region's annual precipitation. In fact, seasonal weather in the Sierra Nevada is more varied and dramatic than in any other mountain range in North America, which has profound implications for the plants and animals living there.

After surviving summer droughts and deep winter snows, plants and animals must contend with massive runoff in the spring. Three-quarters of the Sierra snowpack melts between April and June, and the combined outflow of streams and rivers tumbling down from the Sierra Nevada is often 10 times larger than the Colorado River, which drains seven western states. But precipitation is highly variable. Runoff in very wet years can be up to *20 times* greater than runoff in very dry years.

Although thousands of streams flow down from the Sierra Nevada, they coalesce into 11 major rivers on the mountains' western slope. Yosemite is home to two of the Sierra Nevada's most impressive rivers: the Merced and the Tuolumne, which drain 511 square miles and 680 square miles respectively within the park. All told, over 1,600 miles of streams flow through Yosemite.

Many of Yosemite's streams are fed by high elevation lakes, but these lakes generally support few plants and animals due to a lack of nutrients. Alpine lakes are considered biologically poor because surrounding vegetation is sparse and organic debris is limited. Some alpine lakes have a striking turquoise color, however, due to glacial flour—extremely fine rock particles ground down by glaciers. Glacial flour is flushed into high elevation lakes where, suspended in the otherwise clear water, it reflects blue and green light wavelengths.

At lower elevations with more vegetation, lakes are richer with organic debris, and thus support a thriving food chain. But over time, as organic debris accumulates and tributary streams deposit additional sediments, the lakes ultimately fill in. Many low elevation meadows are former lakes that filled with sediment and organic debris, and many of those meadows will ultimately be invaded by saplings and trees. This successional process has turned many former lakes into meadows and forests—including a massive prehistoric lake that once existed in Yosemite Valley.

But not all meadows will turn into forests. Some meadows exist due to naturally soggy soil conditions that prevent the growth of trees. And though meadows only constitute 3 percent of Yosemite's total area, they are often hotspots of biodiversity. Studies indicate that up to a third of Yosemite plant species occur in meadows, including a new species of orchid, named the Yosemite bog orchid, which was discovered in 2003. Meadows also provide valuable habitats for mammals such as mule deer, Belding's ground squirrels, and pocket gophers.

Although soil fertility in the Sierra Nevada is generally poor due to the short, dry growing season, the mountains are perfect for conifers. Most of the bedrock in the Sierra Nevada is granite, which breaks down into soil that is coarse-grained and granular. As a result, soil throughout much of the Sierra Nevada is thin, rocky and dry, which favors conifers such as lodgepole pines and ponderosa pines. All told, nearly half of all trees in the Sierra Nevada are conifers. By comparison, conifers represent just 10% of trees in the Southeastern U.S.

Today roughly 90 percent of the Sierra Nevada is covered in vegetation. Forests dominate Yosemite's scenery from the park's lowest elevations up to treeline, which occurs at roughly 10,400 feet. Treeline is determined by a number of factors—soil, precipitation, wind, length of growing season—but its limiting factor is cold. If a certain area is too cold, no tree will survive, no matter how favorable the other conditions.

Surprisingly, it's not winter cold but summer cold that determines treeline. Although Sierra trees can survive below average winter temperatures, they cannot withstand those temperatures year-round. Summer temperatures must average 50° F or greater for a tree to grow. If a certain location experiences average July temperatures below 50° F, no trees will grow there.

Treeline is a loose boundary, however, with short scraggly trees finding a way to scrape out a living above 10,400 feet. Some trees grow at dwarf sizes. Others put down roots in warm microclimates that allow them to grow at slightly higher elevations. The absolute limit of treeline, above which no tree can possibly grow, is called the krummholz limit (*krummholz* is the German word for "twisted tree"). In Yosemite, whitebark pine dominates treeline, along with shrubs such as willows, buckwheats, and currants.

Above treeline is the alpine zone—a harsh, beautiful landscape filled with the Sierra's famous sparkling granite. The Sierra Nevada alpine zone stretches over 150 unbroken miles from Mt. Whitney to Sonora Pass, just north of Yosemite. Many hikers and backpackers consider this region to be the most spectacular part of Yosemite, but heavy snow covers the landscape for most of the year, making it accessible only in the summer and fall.

Due to the alpine zone's short growing season, plants growing there flower and fruit much faster than their low-elevations counterparts. As a result, their reproductive cycle is condensed into weeks instead of months. Plants are very active during the summer, photosynthesizing rapidly during the long, sunny days before cold temperatures descend in the fall. Animals in the alpine zone have also adapted to the inhospitable landscape. Many alpine mammals have thick fur and rounded bodies that maximize volume and minimize heat loss. But when winter arrives, most animals in the alpine zone descend to lower, warmer elevations in search of food. Only a few hardy animals remain in the alpine zone year-round.

HUMAN IMPACT

WHEN EUROPEANS FIRST arrived in the Sierra Nevada, they marveled at the sunny, open forests they encountered. Trees were spaced widely apart, and the forest floor was relatively free of debris. According to one early report, you could ride a horse at full gallop through the forest. Unknown to the Europeans, these beautiful, open landscapes were the result of frequent fires.

Small fires caused by lightning strikes historically swept through Sierra Nevada forests about once every decade. These regular fires played an important role in the forest ecosystem, clearing out brush and debris, returning nutrients to the soil, killing insect pests, and destroying saplings that would otherwise compete with older trees. Large trees, protected by thick bark, not only survived the small fires, they thrived in the fire's nutrient-rich wake. In the course of a typical year, it was not uncommon for thousands of acres to burn in the Sierra Nevada. It has been estimated that, historically, roughly 16,000 of Yosemite's 749,000 acres burned each year.

Indians also set intentional fires to maintain open forests and meadows. This reduced the buildup of underbrush and saplings, which could otherwise fuel large wildfires that could destroy mature trees. In some areas, this was of critical importance. The loss of acorn-producing oak trees, for example, would devastate a tribe's annual food supply. Intentional fires also created optimum habitat for animals like deer that the Indians liked to hunt, and open spaces created by fire made hunting much easier. To the Indians, fire was a powerful landscaping tool.

When Indian populations were decimated by disease and genocide, Indian-set fires became increasingly rare. Then, in the mid-1800s, sheepherders began setting frequent fires in the Sierra Nevada to keep meadows open and increase the number of edible grasses for grazing animals. According to one sheepherder, "We started setting fires and continued setting them until we reached the foothills. We burned everything that would burn."

By the late 1890s, when Yosemite and Sequoia National Parks were established, the federal government established a policy of fire suppression to preserve and protect the landscape. The way they saw it, fire marred the scenery, threatened wildlife, and contaminated watersheds. Although the wisdom of fire suppression was questioned by some, it became the dominant forest management policy for the next half century.

Government sponsored fire suppression, combined with the disappearance of Indian-set fires, radically transformed forests in the Sierra Nevada. In some places, natural burning of some species was reduced by 98 percent. As a result, many previously open forests became choked with thick brush and young saplings. Eventually a shady canopy developed that allowed shade-loving trees such as white fir and incense cedar to invade the landscape. Saplings also invaded

CALIFORNIA GRIZZLIES

Prior to European contact, grizzly bears were abundant throughout California. Highly adaptable, their range covered most of the state, excluding the High Sierra and the eastern deserts. "It was not uncommon to see thirty to forty a day," noted one man in the Sacramento Valley in 1841. By 1922, however, not a single grizzly bear remained in

California. The state's entire grizzly population, once estimated at nearly 10,000 bears, had been killed by hunters.

Grizzlies are the largest and most powerful bear in North America, weighing up to 1,500 pounds. They are omnivores that require vast quantities of food on a daily basis, and they will eat plants, animals, insects, and just about anything else they can find. When missions and ranches were established in California in the 1600s, many grizzlies found it easier to kill cattle and other livestock than to hunt wild food. Before long, bored Mexican ranchers were capturing live grizzlies for bull-and-bear fights, where the two animals, tethered together, fought to the death. The grizzly generally won the first round, at which point the ranchers tied up a new bull. Such spectacles supposedly influenced New York newspaper editor Horace Greeley to coin the terms Bull Market and Bear Market, because the bull—or more accurately *bulls*—always won.

During the Bear Flag Revolt of 1846, Americans revolted against Mexican authorities in California. After a swift victory, the Americans raised a new flag that featured a grizzly bear. The flag had a brief career, however, flying less than a month before it was replaced by the stars and stripes. A modified version of the Bear Flag (above) was adopted as California's official state flag in 1911. By that point, however, few grizzlies remained. The last known grizzly in Yosemite was shot in 1895, and the last known grizzly in California was killed in Sequoia National Forest in 1922.

mountain meadows, which had historically been kept open by fire. By the 1940s, much of the Sierra Nevada was overgrown and, in many ways, unnatural.

Although a handful of researchers who studied forest fires in the 1930s concluded that fire was beneficial and necessary, their work did not influence official forest policy. Then, in the 1950s and 60s, researchers realized the severity of the problem at hand. According to one government report, "Today, much of the west slope [of the Sierra] is a dog-hair thicket of young pines, white fir, and incense cedar, and mature brush—a direct function of overprotection from natural fires."

The overgrown forests had reduced habitat for many woodland animals, and the massive amount of water consumed by the new vegetation reduced stream flows and lowered water tables. Perhaps most alarming, the new growth had the potential to fuel massive fires that could destroy mature trees. Many Sierra Nevada forests were, quite literally, sitting on a tinderbox.

Starting in the late 1960s, government officials authorized a regiment of closely monitored prescribed burns in southern Sierra forests. The burns duplicated the small natural fires of the past, reduced fire hazards, diversified habitat, returned nutrients to the soil, and allowed fire-adapted plants to regrow. The burns were a success, and in 1968 prescribed burns were initiated in Yosemite and Sequoia.

Today prescribed burns are an important part of returning Sierra Nevada forests to their natural state. Burns are closely monitored, and they are conducted only when conditions are safe. The park service also allows natural, lightning-caused fires to burn, although they are closely monitored to ensure that they don't grow out of control. Ultimately, it will take decades to return the forests to their natural state. When the damage inflicted by decades of fire suppression has finally been minimized, natural fires will once again maintain the landscape in Yosemite, much as they did for thousands of years.

Disruption of the Sierra Nevada's natural fire patterns is the most dramatic change wrought by European settlers, but the ecosystem has also been altered in less obvious ways. When white settlers arrived in Yosemite in the mid-1800s, there were no fish above 6,000 feet due to natural barriers such as waterfalls and steep gradients. Then, in the late 1800s, trout and other non-natives were intentionally introduced to dozens of lakes in Yosemite. In the early days, fish were placed in 10-gallon milk cans and hauled up the mountains by mule. Later, fish were dropped from planes into mountain lakes.

Introduced fish made tasty meals for anglers but disrupted native ecosystems. The populations of many amphibian species declined as the new arrivals feasted on frogs and tadpoles. Although fish stocking was halted in Yosemite in the 1980s, trout continue to thrive in many high altitude lakes—and amphibian populations continue to decline. A recent drop in mountain yellow-legged frog populations has also been attributed to the deadly chytrid fungus, which has been linked to declining amphibian populations worldwide.

Prescribed Burn

YOSEMITE WILDFLOWERS

Harlequin Lupine
Lupinus stiversii

Mountain Pride Penstemon
Penstemon newberryi

Small Leopard Lily
Lilium parvum

Wild Iris
Iris missouriensis

Pink Monkey Flower
Mimulus lewisii

Coville's Columbine
Aquilegia pubescens

Little Elephants Head
Pedicularis attolens

Shooting Star
Dodecatheon jeffreyi

Sierra Rein Orchid
Habenaria dilatata

Mariposa Lily
Calochortus leichtlinii

Indian Paintbrush
Castilleja miniata

Rockfringe
Epilobium obcordatum

VEGETATIVE ZONES

FOOTHILL WOODLANDS (500 - 3,000 feet)

The foothill woodlands, found only at Yosemite's lowest elevations, are hot and dry in the summer, and winter brings little or no snow. Common plants include manzanita, interior live oak, Douglas oak, gray pine, and many drought-resistant shrubs collectively called chaparral. (The word chaparral is derived from the Spanish *chaparro* "scrub oak.") The foothill woodlands are well adapted to natural fire, passing through frequent cycles of burning and regrowth.

LOWER MONTANE FOREST (3,000 - 6,000 feet)

Lower montane forests cover 166,000 acres in Yosemite, including Yosemite Valley, Wawona, and Big Oak Flat Road. This zone experiences hot, dry summers and cool winters that often bring several feet of snow. Dry slopes are dominated by ponderosa pine, while wet slopes harbor white fir. Other species include sugar pine, incense cedar, black oak, and giant sequoia. Frequent natural fires historically favored the development of ponderosa-dominated forests throughout the lower montane zone.

UPPER MONTANE FOREST (6,000 - 8,000 feet)

This zone, covering 216,000 acres in Yosemite, is characterized by cool summers and cold, snowy winters. Typical trees include pure stands of red fir and lodgepole pine. Other species include western juniper and Jeffrey pine (which has bark that smells like vanilla or butterscotch). The upper montane forest is also noteworthy for its gorgeous meadows filled with blooming wildflowers between June and August.

SUBALPINE SIERRA NEVADA (8,000 - 10,400 feet)

This is Yosemite's largest vegetative zone, covering 297,000 acres. It's also the official start of the High Sierra, defined as the region above 8,000 feet. The subalpine zone is characterized by short, cool summers and long, snowy winters. Tree species include lodgepole pine, mountain hemlock, western white pine, and white bark pine. Lightning strikes are common, but large fires are rare due to the short fire season and frequent natural fire breaks such as meadows and rock outcrops.

ALPINE SIERRA NEVADA (10,400 - 13,000 feet)

Covering 54,300 acres above treeline in Yosemite, the alpine Sierra Nevada is a harsh, rocky landscape where snow covers the ground for most of the year. Summer is measured in weeks, and only hardy plants flourish during the brief growing season. Compared to other alpine areas of comparable latitude in North America, the Sierra Nevada alpine zone is drier than most in the summer, wetter than most in the winter, and warmer than most throughout the year.

COMMON TREES

PONDEROSA PINE
(Pinus ponderosa)

Ponderosa pines are the most common western conifer, with a distribution that roughly outlines the American West. In the central Sierra Nevada they grow at elevations between 3,000 and 6,000 feet, and mature trees can attain heights of 225 feet. Needles grow in bunches of three. The ponderosa's defining characteristic is its pale yellowish bark, which forms large interlocking plates that can look like pieces of a jigsaw puzzle.

INCENSE CEDAR
(Calocedrus decurrens)

Incense cedars, distinguished by their thick, stringy bark, grow up to 150 feet tall. Needles are small, flat, and waxy. The tree's fragrant wood is famous for its use in pencils. A highly versatile conifer, it is able to germinate and grow in both sunny and shady areas. Although once scarce in Yosemite Valley, several decades of fire suppression have allowed incense cedars to flourish.

LODGEPOLE PINE
(Pinus contorta)

Lodgepole pines (named by Lewis & Clark, who observed Indians using them to build lodges) can grow up to 125 feet high. Needles grow in bunches of two. Lodgepoles generally grow between 6,000 and 10,000 feet in the central Sierra Nevada, but occasionally they are found at lower elevations, including Yosemite Valley. The tree's cornflake-like bark flakes off in scales and is among the thinnest of any pine.

GIANT SEQUOIA
(Sequoiadendron giganteum)

Yosemite is a park filled with superlatives, but the giant sequoia (*sequoiadendron giganteum*) remains an unforgettable sight. Capable of weighing over two million pounds, they're not only the largest organisms on earth, they're the largest organisms that have *ever* lived on earth. Reaching a maximum height of 320 feet, sequoias are not the tallest trees in the world (coastal redwoods can grow up to 370 feet), but in terms of mass, the giant sequoia reigns supreme. The base of a mature sequoia can reach over 35 feet in diameter.

Giant sequoias can live up to 3,200 years. Virtually imperishable, mature trees are immune to almost all known pests and diseases. The most common cause of death is toppling over. Although the tree's thick, spongy bark is extremely fire-resistant, the green crown is flammable. That said, up to 90% of the crown can be damaged by fire and the tree will continue to grow. When fire damage disrupts the trunk's water supply, the top of the tree dies back in response, leaving behind a "snag top" common on many older trees. Fire is ultimately beneficial to the tree, however, for the heat of a fire causes cones to dry out and release their seeds. On average, small natural fires sweep through giant sequoia groves every 15 years.

Mature giant sequoias have up to 11,000 cones, and each cone contains about 200 tiny seeds weighing less than 1/5,000 of an ounce. But the odds of a seed growing into an adult tree are outrageously slim. Seedlings require an ideal set of circumstances: recently burned soil, sunny open space (often provided by fire), and access to abundant water. Even if every one of those conditions is met, over 99% of seedlings will die within their first two years. Those that do survive grow tall and pointy for the first 100 years, then develop a rounded crown over the next few centuries. Giant sequoias reach a maximum height around 800 years, and past that age they only grow outward as they continue to add bulk.

Giant sequoias first appeared roughly 175 million years ago during the age of dinosaurs. They are members of the redwood family, which are found only in the U.S. and Asia. Giant sequoias are found exclusively on the western slope of the Sierra Nevada, occupying a range only 260 miles long by 15 miles wide. There are 75 known groves, and they generally occur between 5,000 and 7,000 feet. There are three giant sequoia groves in Yosemite (p.74, 74). Local Indians supposedly called the giant trees *wah-wo-nah*, an imitation of a hooting owl, which was considered the guardian spirit of the trees. The name "sequoia" is derived, strangely enough, from the Cherokee Indian Sequoyah, who developed a written version of his people's language.

Giant
Sequoia

Blue
Whale

Human

Peregrine Falcon
Falco peregrinus

Peregrine falcons are among the world's most formidable birds of prey. They can spot victims from thousands of feet above, then dive bomb them at speeds topping 200 mph—the fastest speed of any animal. Victims that don't die upon impact have their necks broken by the peregrine's powerful beak. Peregrine falcons are such successful strikers that they were used to kill Nazi carrier pigeons in World War II. By the early 1970s, however, U.S. populations had plummeted due to the toxic effects of the pesticide DDT. To save the remaining birds, young peregrines were captured, bred in captivity, and reintroduced into the wild. Peregrines nest on tall cliffs, and from February–August several cliffs in Yosemite are off-limits to rock climbers to protect nesting falcons. In 1999 peregrines were removed from the federal Endangered Species list. In 2009 they were removed from California's endangered species list.

Steller's Jay
Cyanocitta stelleri

These pretty blue birds are common in Yosemite, particularly when food is present—as any picnic lover can attest. Stellar's jays are found at high elevations throughout the western U.S., and their range extends from Alaska to Nicaragua. Closely related to blue jays, they are distinguished by a black head and upper body. Their call is a harsh, descending *shaaaar*. Steller's jays also imitate the cries of predators such as red-tailed hawks, a trick they use to scare away other birds from feeding areas. Along with crows and magpies, jays are considered among the world's most intelligent birds. Steller's jays are omnivores that eat pine nuts, fruits, seeds, insects, bird eggs and even young birds. In autumn they can harvest up to 400 acorns per hour. Stellar's jays are found in Yosemite year-round. They typically live in flocks of ten or more, but they must constantly stay alert for goshawks, which snatch them with vice-like talons. Steller's jays are named after the German naturalist Georg Steller, who first recorded them in 1741.

Western Tanager
Piranga ludoviciana

Members of the cardinal family, western tanagers are famous for the male's vibrant breeding plumage. During breeding season the males' bright red face and yellow breast are contrasted by dark black wings. Females are far less showy, with a drab olive coloration. Like all cardinals western tanagers are classified as songbirds. Their call has been described as a hoarse, monotonous *pit-er-ick.* Their summer breeding range covers much of western North America, extending from northern Mexico to Alaska. Western tanagers build flimsy cup nests in horizontal branches. They typically lay four bluish-green eggs with brown spots. Their nests are preyed upon by Clark's nutcrackers and Stellar's jays, and adult tanagers are preyed upon by hawks and falcons. The western tanager's winter range extends from central Mexico to Costa Rica, where they are often seen in coffee plantations. They migrate alone or in groups of up to 30 birds. The majority of their diet consists of insects, but they also feed on berries and fruits.

Great Gray Owl
Strix nebulosa

Great gray owls are the world's largest owl species by length, measuring up to 33 inches long with a five-foot wingspan. Due to their large size they have few natural predators. They hunt small rodents such as voles and shrews. In winter great gray owls use exceptional hearing to detect animals burrowing under two feet of snow, then "snow-plunge" their prey. Rather than build their own nests, great gray owls often use the abandoned nests of large birds such as raptors. Although the vast majority of great gray owls live in Canada and Russia, an isolated population of 200-300 owls lives in the Sierra Nevada Mountains. This genetically distinct sub species, *Strix nebulosa Yosemitensis*, is listed under California's endangered species act. Roughly 65% of California's great gray owls reside in Yosemite, which marks the southern limit of their range.

Black Bears

Ursus americanus

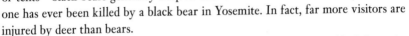

No animal in Yosemite is as famous—or as infamous—as the black bear. Their large size, sharp claws and powerful limbs stir up feelings of fear and dread in many visitors, but black bears are actually quite docile. Unless threatened or provoked—or offered the opportunity to steal human food from cars or tents—black bears generally keep to themselves. No one has ever been killed by a black bear in Yosemite. In fact, far more visitors are injured by deer than bears.

There are roughly 22,000 black bears in California and 400 black bears in Yosemite. Despite their name, California black bears are generally dark brown or cinnamon colored. Their name comes from bears in the eastern U.S. and Pacific Northwest, where the species sports a rich black coat. In Yosemite, the bears' light coloration has led some visitors to mistake them for grizzly bears, which are also brown. Although grizzly bears historically roamed the Sierra Nevada, they were eliminated by hunters nearly a century ago (p.65).

Of the three bear species in North America—black, grizzly and polar—black bears are the smallest and most common. They grow up to five feet long and three feet high at the shoulder. In Yosemite black bears generally weigh between 200 and 350 pounds. The largest bear ever captured in the park weighed 690 pounds. Despite their roly poly appearance, black bears can reach top speeds of 30 mph over short distances. They are also excellent tree climbers.

Black bears are omnivores that eat just about anything—grass in the spring, berries in the summer, acorns in the fall. Roughly 80% of their diet is vegetation, but they also eat ants, termites and insect larvae. In autumn black bears consume up to 20,000 calories per day in preparation for hibernation. But black bears are not true hibernators. After snuggling into their dens in October or November, they enter a "light" hibernation referred to as Seasonal Lethargy. During this time a black bear's heartbeat drops from 60 to 80 beats per minute to as low as eight beats per minute. Compared to true hibernators, a black bear's body temperature drops relatively little. During winter dormancy, which lasts three to five months, bears lose roughly 25–30% of their body weight.

Black bears live about 18 years in the wild. The oldest known bear in Yosemite was 28 years old. Between the ages of three and five, females

Black Bear Range

produce their first offspring, and they breed about every two years after that. Mating occurs in the summer, but embryos do not develop until the mother has put on adequate weight to survive the winter. Cubs, which weigh less than a pound at birth, are born in late January/early February while the mother is still in her den. Most litters consist of one to three cubs. Young bears stay with their mother for a full year while they learn to fend for themselves.

Black bears have relatively poor eyesight, but they have exceptionally good hearing and smell. They are highly intelligent and adaptable. Unfortunately, some Yosemite black bears have changed their natural behavior in response to a new delicacy: human food. The problem began in the 1920s, when Yosemite's bears discovered the pleasure of eating garbage. Instead of discouraging this behavior, the park service established an open air dump where the bears could feast. They then installed bleachers and stadium lighting so visitors could watch the nightly "Bear Show."

Although Bear Shows ended in 1940, bears continued to seek out human food. As more and more people flooded into Yosemite, conflicts between bears and people grew increasingly common. Bears that repeatedly raided food from cars and tents were deemed "corrupted," and corrupted bears were killed. Before long, hundreds of bears had been killed in Yosemite.

Starting in the 1970s, the park service took a new approach. Rather than try to manage bear behavior, they took steps to manage human behavior. "Bear proof" trash cans and food lockers were placed throughout the park, and visitors were handed pamphlets with instructions on proper food storage. Although these efforts have been successful, improper food storage by visitors remains the number one cause of human-bear conflicts in the park. (For more on proper food storage, see p.74).

Mule Deer

Odocoileus hemionus

Mule deer are named for their large ears, which move independently of each other like those of a mule. They are common throughout the western U.S., and their range extends from western Canada to central Mexico. Adult mule deer are five to seven feet long. Bucks weigh 150 to 300 pounds. Does weigh 95 to 200 pounds.

Mule deer are ruminants with multi-chambered stomachs. In the summer they forage on plants, leaves and brushy vegetation. In the winter they forage on conifers such as juniper and ponderosa pine. Although closely related to white-tailed deer, mule deer are slightly larger. Mule deer also have white tails with a black tip and bifurcated antlers that "fork" as they grow. (White-tailed deer antlers, by contrast, branch from a single main beam.) Bucks grow a large pair of antlers each year, then shed them each winter. The annual cycle of antler growth and shedding is regulated by changes in the length of the day.

During the fall rut (mating season), bucks compete for females. Although conflict between bucks is infrequent, mild fights sometimes break out. Fighting bucks enmesh antlers, then try to force the head of the other buck down. Although injuries are rare, antlers sometimes become locked together. If the two bucks cannot unlock their antlers, they will be unable to eat, and both will ultimately die of starvation.

After breeding in the fall, gestation lasts 190 to 200 days. Young does give birth to one fawn. Older does often give birth to twins. Fawns are born with white spots on their backs, which help camouflage them with the dappled light of the forest floor. As fawns grow older, the white spots disappear. Fawns are able to distinguish their mother through a unique odor produced by glands on the mother's hind legs. Fawns stay with their mother until they are weaned in the fall. Conflict between does is common, so family groups tend to be spaced widely apart.

Adult mule deer live up to eleven years in the wild. Their main predators in Yosemite are mountain lions and coyotes.

Mule Deer
Range

Mountain Lion
Felis concolor

Mountain lions (also known as pumas, cougars or catamounts) are found from Canada to Argentina—the most extensive range of any mammal in the Western Hemisphere. Historically they inhabited all 48 lower U.S. states, but in the late 1800s and early 1900s mountain lions were hunted to the brink of extinction. Following the enactment of strict hunting regulations, they have made a steady comeback in the West. Today mountain lions are once again spreading east.

Mountain lions are the second-largest wildcats in the Western Hemisphere after jaguars. Males weigh up to 250 pounds and can measure more than eight feet in length. Females weigh up to 140 pounds and measure up to seven feet in length. Mountain lions have proportionally the largest hind legs of any feline. They can jump nearly 20 feet vertically, 30 feet horizontally, and reach top speeds of 50 mph. Retractable claws aid in both hunting and tree climbing.

Mountain lions, like all felines, require meat to survive. They travel up to 25 miles a day in search of food. Mountain lions are quick, efficient hunters, quietly stalking prey before pouncing. Victims often die from a lethal bite to the spinal cord. In Yosemite mountain lions feed primarily on mule deer, coyote and bighorn sheep. If those animals are unavailable, mountain lions hunt small rodents, lizards and birds.

Solitary and territorial, mountain lions require an extensive "home range" that can measure up to 185 square miles. Adult mountain lions come together only to mate. Females are exclusively responsible for parenting, and cubs stay with their mother for roughly two years while she teaches them survival skills. Mountain lions are born with a spotted coloration. They develop a uniform tan coloration by about 2.5 years in age.

Reclusive by nature, mountain lions go to great lengths to avoid people. Sightings are uncommon, and attacks on humans are extremely rare. If you do encounter a mountain lion in Yosemite, slowly back away while holding a steady gaze.

Mountain
Lion Range

Coyote
Canis latrans

Nocturnal by nature, coyotes are seldom seen during the day, but their haunting howls often echo through Yosemite at night. One long, high-pitched howl calls a pack of coyotes together. When the pack has gathered, a cacophony of yips and yelps are added to the mix.

Today coyotes range from Canada to Panama, but historically they were confined to the western U.S. and Mexico. Following the extermination of wolves in the 1800s, coyotes spread rapidly throughout North America. Intelligent, adaptable animals with a knack for scavenging, coyote populations have held steady and even increased in some places despite years of being hunted, poisoned and trapped. This is partly due to an amazing reproductive adaptation: when coyotoe populations decline, the remaining coyotes produce larger litters.

Coyotes are distant relatives of gray wolves. The two species diverged in North America roughly two million years ago. Coyotes travel in packs of six or so family members, and their diet, which is 90% animal-based, consists mostly of rodents and small mammals. Coyotes eat just about anything, however, including birds, snakes, insects and trash. Working in teams, coyotes sometimes hunt large animals such as deer. While pursuing prey, they can reach speeds of 40 mph and jump up to 13 feet.

Coyotes are strictly monogamous. They mate in the winter, and mothers give birth to an average of six pups in the spring. Young coyotes are extremely vulnerable. Up to two-thirds of pups do not survive to adulthood. Coyotes that reach adulthood often live 10 years or more in the wild. Adults weigh up to 40 pounds and can grow up to four feet in length. In Yosemite mountain lions are coyotes' only natural predator.

Coyotes play a prominent role in the legends of native tribes. Among a small cast of human and animal characters, Coyote is portrayed as a scheming trickster who scrapes by on cunning and charm. The word "coyote" is derived from the Nahuatl (Aztec) word *cóyotl*. In Aztec culture coyotes were revered as a symbol of military might. Coyote's Latin name, *Canis latrans*, means "barking dog," a reference to its famous howl.

Coyote
Range

Bighorn Sheep

Ovis canadensis

Bighorn sheep are among Yosemite's most impressive animals. Well adapted to alpine terrain, they can traverse two-inch ledges, scramble up steep slopes and jump down 20-foot inclines with grace. Their unique concave hooves, which feature a hard outer edge and soft interior sole, help them grip rocks and navigate cliffs. John Muir was so impressed with bighorn climbing skills that he dubbed them "animal mountaineers."

The ram's legendary horns take up to a decade to grow, curving up and over the ears in a C-shaped curl. A large pair of horns can weigh up to 30 pounds and reach 30 inches in length. During mating season, competing rams charge each other head on at speeds topping 20 mph. When rams collide, their horns smash together, producing a loud cracking sound that can be heard for miles. Thickened skulls allow rams to withstand repeated collisions. Rams can fight for over 24 hours, and those with the biggest horns generally do the most mating.

Bighorn rams weigh up to 220 pounds. Ewes weigh up to 160 pounds. Both rams and ewes develop horns shortly after birth, but ewe horns are skinny and never grow past half curl. Ewes generally stay with their family herd. Adult rams, by contrast, live largely isolated lives. In the Sierra Nevada, bighorn sheep live at elevations between 10,000 and 14,000 feet.

Sierra Nevada bighorn sheep (*Ovis canadensis sierrae*) are one of three bighorn subspecies. The other two are Rocky Mountain bighorn sheep and Desert bighorn sheep. Prior to European settlement, several thousand bighorn sheep roamed the Sierra Nevada. By 1979, however, the Sierra bighorn population had fallen to barely 100 individuals due to hunting and diseases transmitted from domestic sheep. A bighorn recovery program has since established several new herds, including one in Yosemite's Cathedral Range. Today there are roughly 400 bighorn sheep in the Sierra Nevada.

Bighorn
Sheep Range

Yellow-Bellied Marmot

Marmota flaviventris

These roly-poly alpine critters are one of the High Sierra's most lovable sights. Western cousins of *Marmota monax* (better known as groundhogs or woodchucks) marmots are often seen perched high on a rock, taking in their surroundings or basking in the summer sun. Marmots are generally found above 6,500 feet in the western U.S. and Canada, and they are common in the Sierra Nevada.

Despite their yellow-bellied name, marmots won't think twice about grabbing your lunch. During the short summer season marmots are aggressive food opportunists, eating as much as possible and packing on thick layers of fat to survive the harsh winter that lies ahead. Their diet includes leaves, grasses, berries, flowers, insects and birds' eggs. By the time autumn rolls around, male marmots, which are larger than females, can weigh up to 11.5 pounds.

Marmots are deep hibernators, spending up to eight months in hibernation in dens up to 23 feet deep. During this time their metabolic rate slows down by as much as two-thirds. While hibernating their heartbeat drops from 100 beats per minute to four beats per minute, their body temperature drops from 97°F to 40°F, and they breathe only once every *six minutes*.

After emerging from their hibernation den in the spring, male marmots dig a new, smaller den under a pile of rocks. This new den, which typically measures 3 feet deep, keeps them safe from predators such as mountain lions and coyotes. Each male then gathers a harem of up to four females to live in his den. Marmots have a "harem-polygynous" mating system where a male defends multiple females. Marmots form colonies of 10 to 20 individuals. When one marmot spots a predator, it emits a loud whistle to warn other marmots of the danger.

Marmot Range

Female marmots have litters of three to five pups, but only about half of those pups will survive their first year. Young females typically remain in their home area, while yearling males leave in search of available females. Marmots reproduce around two years of age. Adult marmots can live up to 15 years.

Little Brown Bat

Myotis lucifugus

Little brown bats are one of 17 bat species found in Yosemite. Their wingspans measure up to 10.5 inches wide, yet they weigh just 0.5 ounces. Like all bats they use echolocation, a technique similar to radar, to find insects such as wasps and mosquitos. While in flight little brown bats emit 20 high pitched calls per second. When they detect prey, they emit up to 200 calls per second. These calls, which have a frequency of 40-80 kHz, are beyond the range of human hearing. Upon reaching an insect swarm little brown bats use their wings to scoop the bugs into their mouths. A single bat can consume up to 1,200 insects each night. Little brown bats undergo a daily "torpor," or sleep state, which can last up to 20 hours. They are most active at dusk and dawn. In the summer, males and females live apart while females raise the young. In the winter, both sexes migrate south and hibernate together.

Belding's Ground Squirrel

Spermophilus beldingi

These adorable ground squirrels live in alpine meadows above 5,000 feet. When not nibbling on grasses and flowers, they often sit erect on their haunches, earning them the nickname "picket pin" squirrel. Belding's ground squirrels hibernate seven to eight months—one of the longest hibernation periods of any North American mammal. To prepare for their long hibernation, they eat voraciously throughout the summer, doubling their weight by autumn and increasing their body fat by a factor of 15. Males emerge from hibernation about two weeks before females, tunneling through snow to reach the surface. Females emerge when the snow has melted. Within six days females are ready to mate, but they will only mate on a single day during a window that lasts just three to six hours. Not surprisingly, competition for females is extremely fierce during this window. Fighting among males is common, and injuries can be fatal. Females mate with several males, then give birth to a litter about one month later. By late August male pups have moved away from their birthplace. Females stay where they were born, and multiple female generations often share an ancestral site.

HISTORY

THE FIRST PEOPLE to set eyes on Yosemite were the Miwok Indians, who lived throughout the central Sierra Nevada for thousands of years. To the Indians, Yosemite Valley must have seemed like paradise on earth: a fortress-like hideaway filled with fresh water, edible plants, and wild game. They called the Valley *Ahwahnee*, "Place Like A Gaping Mouth," and the Miwok living there were called the *Ahwahneechee*, "People of the Ahwahnee."

The Valley's abundant natural resources supported roughly 200 people—a fraction of the estimated 100,000 Indians living throughout the Sierra Nevada, but a relatively large number for a single location. Over 35 Ahwahneechee living sites have been identified in Yosemite Valley, including permanent and temporary villages, as well as seasonal hunting and fishing camps. The largest and most important village, *Koomine*, was located below Yosemite Falls and stretched roughly three-quarters of a mile.

During the hot summer months the Ahwahneechee wore few clothes. Men covered themselves with a single piece of deerskin folded about the hips, women wore a two-piece buckskin skirt, and children went naked until they were about 10 years old. Important villagers decorated themselves with buckskin sashes, and decorated their hair with wildflowers. When temperatures dropped, the Ahwahneechee wrapped themselves in animal-skin robes. Although the Ahwahneechee went barefoot in the village during the warmer months, they wore moccasins lined with cedar bark in the winter. Snowshoes, fashioned out of split saplings, were also used for winter travel in the High Sierra.

Edible plants, gathered by Ahwahneechee women, made up most of the tribe's diet. Greens and bulbs were harvested in the spring, seeds and fruits in the summer, and acorns in the fall. All told, over 100 plant species were harvested. In bountiful years excess crops were dried and placed in storage. In lean years Indians turned to alternate crops and traded for food with neighboring tribes, including the Mono, Yokuts, and Midou. In exchange for Ahwahneechee acorns, berries, baskets, and arrow shafts, the neighboring tribes traded salt, pinyon pine nuts, red pigment for paint, and obsidian (volcanic glass) used for arrowheads.

Although acorns and other wild crops were the tribe's main sources of food, they also hunted wild animals. Hunting was the responsibility of Ahwahneechee males. When hunting alone, Indians often wore a disguise to blend in with the scenery. The most impressive disguise was the entire skin of a buck, complete with antler-shaped twigs, that the hunter wrapped around his body. The disguise, believed to hold magical powers, was put on in secret and kept hidden between hunting ceremonies to avoid contamination by women and children. In the field, the disguised hunter mimicked the movements of a deer until he was accepted by a herd.

In their free time, both men and women played a sport similar to lacrosse with basket rackets and a buckskin ball shot through willow goal posts. Villagers also gambled on archery tournaments, footraces, and spear throwing contests. Ceremonies and rituals were common throughout the year, and in the spring and the fall special "world-renewing ceremonies" were held to bring rain, maintain bountiful crops, provide animals for hunting, and prevent natural disasters.

According to early Yosemite settler Galen Clark, the Ahwahneechee were polygamists. Women were considered property, and parents sold their young daughters to the highest suitable bidder. Payment for a bride was considered an important part of the marriage ceremony. Wealthy men often had two or three wives, and once married a husband could sell or gamble his wife away—though such occurrences were said to be rare. If a woman was unfaithful to her husband, she was punished with death.

Although generally peaceful, the Ahwahneechee occasionally waged war with neighboring tribes. Galen Clark described them as "perhaps the most warlike of any of the tribes in this part of the Sierra Nevada Mountains, who were, as a rule, a peaceful people." Most disputes were settled through negotiation, but when negotiation failed the tribes resorted to violence.

Ahwahneechee Dwellings

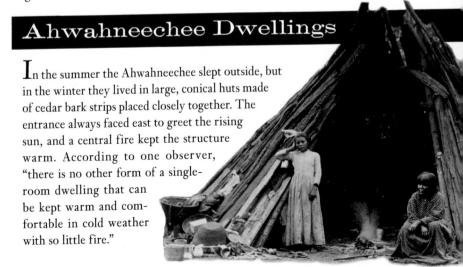

In the summer the Ahwahneechee slept outside, but in the winter they lived in large, conical huts made of cedar bark strips placed closely together. The entrance always faced east to greet the rising sun, and a central fire kept the structure warm. According to one observer, "there is no other form of a single-room dwelling that can be kept warm and comfortable in cold weather with so little fire."

Ahwahneechee Basketry

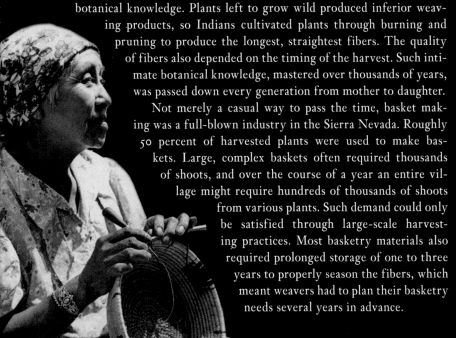

Basket making, a task performed only by women, was one of the most important aspects of Ahwahneechee culture. In the absence of pottery, baskets were essential to daily life. There were dozens of baskets with hundreds of uses: storing food, collecting trash, transporting firewood, trapping fish, etc. Baskets were given as gifts and buried with the dead, and basketry skills helped determine a woman's social status within the tribe. Ahwahneechee women were such skilled weavers that many of their baskets were watertight.

Serving more than just practical needs, basketry was a form of self-expression with important symbolic meanings. Ahwahneechee women wove beautiful baskets decorated with beads and feathers, and top basket makers were as dexterous as professional musicians, often weaving into old age, long after their eyesight had failed. Basketry was a combination of technical skill and encyclopedic botanical knowledge. Plants left to grow wild produced inferior weaving products, so Indians cultivated plants through burning and pruning to produce the longest, straightest fibers. The quality of fibers also depended on the timing of the harvest. Such intimate botanical knowledge, mastered over thousands of years, was passed down every generation from mother to daughter.

Not merely a casual way to pass the time, basket making was a full-blown industry in the Sierra Nevada. Roughly 50 percent of harvested plants were used to make baskets. Large, complex baskets often required thousands of shoots, and over the course of a year an entire village might require hundreds of thousands of shoots from various plants. Such demand could only be satisfied through large-scale harvesting practices. Most basketry materials also required prolonged storage of one to three years to properly season the fibers, which meant weavers had to plan their basketry needs several years in advance.

EUROPEAN DISCOVERY

IN 1542 JUAN Rodríguez Cabrillo sailed north from Mexico to become the first non-Indian to explore California. Just south of present-day Monterrey he spied snow-capped mountains in the distance and described them as *la sierra nevada*, "The Snowy Range." But the mountains he saw were not the present-day Sierra Nevada, which has since led to much confusion in the history of the range. It wasn't until 1776 that Pedro Font, a Spaniard who helped colonize San Francisco Bay, saw the mountains and described them as *una gran sierra nevada*, "A Great Snowy Range." That same year he produced a map of the region, labeling the mountains "Sierra Nevada."

For the next five decades the Sierra Nevada was essentially ignored. As far as the Spanish were concerned, the range was simply a massive barrier to eastern travel, and the Spaniards already had their hands full along the coast. Their Catholic missions were in disarray, and Mexico was threatening to revolt.

Following the Mexican War of Independence (1810-1821), Mexico gained control of California. Around this time American beaver trappers started venturing into California from the east, searching for new hunting grounds away from the overtrapped Rockies. In 1827 legendary fur trapper Jedediah Smith, fresh from blazing an overland route from the Rockies to Southern California, led two companions up and over the western slope of the Sierra Nevada. Just 27 years old, Smith became the first white man to cross the Sierra Nevada, trudging through deep spring snow just north of Yosemite.

Seven years later the U.S. Army dispatched a 58-man expedition to cross the Sierra from the east. Led by 34-year-old Joseph Walker—a man whose "chief delight" was "to explore unknown regions"—the expedition's goal was to gather basic information about California. In mid-October 1833, after leading his men across the Great Basin Desert, Joseph Walker reached the eastern base of the Sierra Nevada. By the time he arrived, winter had already blanketed the mountains in a fresh layer of snow. Undaunted, the men scaled the sheer eastern slope. It was a grueling journey. Deep snow made travel difficult and foraging virtually impossible for the expedition's pack animals. The men, dressed in knee-length buckskin shirts and leather leggings, battled frostbite and starvation as they descended the western slope. As food supplies dwindled, the men were reduced to eating horses that died along the way. "Our situation was growing more distressing every hour," one party member wrote, "and all we now thought of was to extricate ourselves from this inhospitable region."

Pushing on, the men followed a large stream they hoped would lead them to the base of the mountains. After a short distance the stream burst through the forest and plunged over the edge of a sheer cliff. Standing on a rocky precipice, the men became the first non-Indians to set eyes on Yosemite Valley.

Pulling out a spyglass, Walker scanned the surroundings. Yosemite Valley was free of snow and in full autumn glory. Sheer cliffs, granite domes, and dramatic waterfalls towered above open forests and meadows. A sparkling river twisted through the center of the Valley. To the shivering, half-starved men, it seemed like divine intervention—the perfect place to hunt fresh meat and for their horses to graze on tall grasses. For two days the men tried to find a route down the sheer cliffs, but ultimately they concluded that it was "utterly impossible for a man to descend."

Dejected, the men spent three days bushwhacking an alternate route down the mountains. Although Walker's party never entered Yosemite Valley, the fact that they viewed it at all is a miracle. Tucked away in the heart of the Sierra Nevada, guarded on all sides by sheer cliffs and forests, Yosemite Valley is one of the most geographically well-concealed locations in California. In the mid-1800s, you literally had to stumble upon Yosemite Valley to find it—which is exactly what the next white people did.

In October 1849, two gold miners tracked a grizzly bear just south of Yosemite. Bushwhacking through the trees, the men stumbled upon an Indian trail that led them to the entrance of Yosemite Valley. They were spellbound by the scenery. Laid out before them were "stupendous cliffs rising perhaps 3000 feet from their base which gave us cause for wonder." Content simply to savor the view, the two men never entered Yosemite Valley. Had they ventured farther they would have encountered a world virtually unchanged since the Walker expedition. In the years between, however, life just outside the Valley had been turned completely upside down.

THE GOLD RUSH

ON JANUARY 24, 1848, nine days before the U.S. acquired California from Mexico, a man named James Marshall noticed something sparkling in the American River in the foothills northwest of Yosemite. "It made my heart thump," he later recounted, "for I was certain it was gold." Marshall tried to keep his discovery secret, but rumors quickly spread. When local store owner Sam Brannan heard the news, he purchased enormous quantities of mining supplies. He then headed to San Francisco and waved a bottle of gold dust over his head shouting, "Gold! Gold from the American River!" Within a few weeks, 75 percent of the men living in San Francisco had left town to dig for gold.

News of California's instant riches spread like wildfire across the globe. At the start of 1848, 800 people lived in San Francisco. By the end of 1849, 100,000 people had arrived in California, and thousands more were on their way. They came from Europe, China, Australia, South America—anywhere the news spread. In 1850 California demanded statehood and got it. By the end of the decade, over 300,000 people had flooded the state and two million pounds of gold (worth over $15 billion today) had been pulled out of California mines and streams.

In 1848, when miners first arrived in the foothills, local Indians greeted them with characteristic hospitality. Natives watched the mining process with great interest, and when they realized the value of the shiny metal many Indians panned for it themselves. Indians eagerly exchanged gold dust for blankets and other supplies. For a short while, everything was fine.

Then, as tens of thousands of miners poured into the foothills, the situation quickly deteriorated. Miners competed with Indians for deer and chopped down acorn-bearing oak trees—the Indians' primary source of food. Many miners were inherently distrustful of Indians, and they often confiscated Indian territory by force. Within months Indians became second class citizens in a land they had occupied for thousands of years.

Angry and starving, some Indians were reduced to raiding mining camps and trading posts. Such incidents, reported widely among miners, further fueled white suspicion, leading to a downward spiral of white-Indian relations.

Just south of Yosemite, a ruthless, charismatic man named James Savage employed hundreds of Indians to work his lucrative mining claims. A former cattle thief, Savage turned his attention to gold when the news broke, and soon he oversaw a small empire of gold mines and trading posts. By 1850 he was earning roughly $20,000 a day. To ensure the Indians' goodwill, he learned their language, adopted their customs, and married the daughters of several chiefs. He also intimidated the Indians through claims of supernatural powers. According to one story, he once let an Indian shoot at him with a gun filled with six blanks. As each shot went off, Savage made a grabbing gesture in the air. When the smoke cleared, Savage produced six bullets in his hands—proof, he declared, that guns

could not harm him. According to one observer, "Jim Savage was the absolute and despotic ruler over thousands of Indians ... and was by them designated in their Spanish vernacular *El Rey Guero*—the blonde king."

As Savage amassed a small fortune, he grew increasingly flamboyant. His Indian workers, meanwhile, grew increasingly unhappy as they realized he was growing rich at their expense. On a trip to San Francisco with Indian leader José Juarez, Savage visited a gambling hall, jumped up on a table, and bet his weight in gold on a playing card. In an instant he lost $35,000. He paid the debt with money given to him by Indians to purchase supplies. Juarez, outraged, berated Savage in the street. Savage responded by knocking Juarez to the ground.

Word of Savage's exploits quickly spread among his Indian workers, and Savage returned home to a flurry of discontent. With the situation spiraling out of control, Savage called several Indian leaders together. Addressing them in their native tongue, Savage explained that, "If war is made and the white men are aroused to anger, every Indian engaged in war will be killed."

Juarez, still fuming, stated that white men in faraway cities would not help miners fight Indians. But even if they did, "we will go to the mountains. If they follow, they cannot find us. Our country is now overrun with white people; we must fight to protect ourselves."

THE MARIPOSA BATTALION

IN DECEMBER OF 1851, two of Savage's trading posts were raided by angry Indians. Fearful of reprisal, hundreds of Savage's Indian workers fled to the mountains. In response, Savage assembled a 200-man militia called the Mariposa Battalion, with Savage serving as commander.

Before the Battalion could take action, however, federal Indian commissioners arrived and demanded a halt to all hostile activities. Hoping for a diplomatic solution, the commissioners tried to negotiate peace treaties with local tribes. In exchange for leaving the mountains, most "hostile" tribes accepted government land in the Central Valley. But the Ahwahneechee refused. White men had yet to enter Yosemite Valley, and the Ahwahneechee had no interest in leaving their home. A stalemate ensued. The Indian commissioners gave the Indians eight days to leave the mountains, but the Indians stood their ground. With no solution at hand, the Mariposa Battalion was sent to Yosemite Valley.

At the time, the Ahwahneechee were led by a powerful chief named Tenaya, who had only recently led his people back to Yosemite. Several decades earlier, a terrible plague had swept through the mountains, and Yosemite Valley was abandoned. The survivors, including Tenaya's father, fled to the desert at the eastern base of the Sierra to live with the Mono Indians. Tenaya's father took a Mono wife, and Tenaya was raised among her people, listening to stories of the old days in Yosemite Valley. When Tenaya was a young man, an old shaman urged him to leave the desert and reestablish his people in the mountains. Sometime around 1821, Tenaya returned to Yosemite Valley with 200 followers.

Now, having recently reclaimed their homeland, the Ahwahneechee were confronted with a new threat. As the Mariposa Battalion approached Yosemite Valley, Tenaya headed down to meet with Savage. Tenaya asked why the Indians were being expelled from their homeland. Savage explained that the white man would give the Indians everything they needed, including protection.

"We have all we need," Tenaya responded, "we do not want anything from white men … let us remain in the mountains where we were born." Savage was unmoved by the chief's argument. If a treaty is not signed, Savage told Tenaya, "your whole tribe will be destroyed; not one of them will be left alive."

Torn between expulsion and war, Tenaya reluctantly surrendered. A few days later, roughly 70 Ahwahneechee trudged out of the mountains through deep snow. But Savage believed many Indians remained hiding in the mountains, so he continued on to Yosemite Valley with roughly 60 Battalion members.

On March 27, 1851, the soldiers reached an overlook with breathtaking views of Yosemite Valley. The light was soft and a fine mist swirled over the trees. One man in the party, Dr. Lafayette Bunnell, was moved to tears by the scenery. Savage thought Bunnell foolish and ordered him to move on. Descending towards Bridalveil Fall, they became the first white men to enter Yosemite Valley.

The next day the men searched the Valley but found only an abandoned Ahwahneechee village. The remaining Indians had fled to higher elevations, and the Battalion, running low on supplies, was forced to turn around. Making matters worse, Tenaya and the other captive Indians somehow managed to escape in the middle of the night. To Savage, the expedition was a failure. But Bunnell would later write that, "We had discovered, named, and partially explored, one of the most remarkable ... geographical wonders of the world."

A few weeks later, a second expedition was sent to Yosemite Valley, and the Indians were rounded up and marched to the reservation at gunpoint. But life on the reservation was miserable. Tenaya pleaded with his captors to return to Yosemite, and finally he was granted permission to leave. The rest of the tribe quietly followed Tenaya, and no effort was made to bring them back.

Then, in 1852, a group of miners wandered into Yosemite Valley to pan for gold. A skirmish broke out that left two miners dead, and another militia was promptly dispatched to Yosemite. Five Indians were shot and several more were hung from oak trees, but Tenaya, certain that the hostility was not over, ordered his people to cross the Sierras and take shelter with the Mono tribe.

The following year, Tenaya led his people back to Yosemite Valley. According to one story, later that fall a group of young Ahwahneechee stole horses from the Mono without Tenaya's permission. The Mono sent a war party to Yosemite Valley in response, and in the skirmish that followed Tenaya was stoned to death. Many young Ahwahneechee were also killed, and the women and children were taken captive by the Mono and marched back over the Sierra. Only a handful of elderly Ahwahneechee were allowed to remain in Yosemite Valley. From that point forward, traditional Ahwahneechee life would never be the same.

Grizzly Adams

In 1849 a bankrupt Massachusetts shoemaker named James Adams headed to California to try his luck in the Gold Rush. After making and losing several fortunes, Adams grew despondent. "I abandoned all my schemes for wealth," he wrote, "and took the road towards the wildest and most unfrequented parts of the Sierra Nevada, resolved to make the wilderness my home, and wild beasts my companions." In 1856 Adams moved to San Francisco and opened The Mountaineer Museum, which featured elk, eagles, vultures, wildcats, mountain lions, and trained grizzlies that performed tricks. Holding court was Adams himself, dressed in fringed buckskin, moccasins, and a deerskin hat. The museum was a hit, and Adams, who had a knack for publicity, was often seen walking the streets of downtown San Francisco with his grizzlies in tow. His star attraction, Samson, a 1,500 pound grizzly captured in Yosemite, became the model for California's official state flag.

ARTISTS & TOURISTS

AT FIRST, MOST Californians knew nothing of the discovery of Yosemite Valley by the Mariposa Battalion. The foothills were still filled with gold, and miners could think of little else. Then, in 1855, a writer named James Hutchings came across a printed account of the Battalion's expedition. He found himself stunned. The discovery of a thousand foot waterfall—six times higher than world-famous Niagara Falls—was extraordinary news, and it had yet to be widely reported. Hutchings, who was in the midst of launching an illustrated monthly magazine, immediately set off for the mysterious valley.

Hutchings arrived in Yosemite Valley in June with three companions and two Indian guides. The group spent five days exploring the Valley, taking notes, sketching illustrations, and basking in the scenery. Hutchings was beside himself. The springtime glory of Yosemite Valley far exceeded his expectations—the waterfall he had read about was in reality over *two thousand* feet high—and shortly thereafter he wrote a glowing article for a Mariposa newspaper describing the "luxurious scenic banqueting." By the end of the summer, over 40 people had visited Yosemite Valley.

The following year, two enterprising miners opened a 50-mile horse trail to Yosemite, charging $2 per horseback rider. The multi-day ride, which involved steep climbs and sheer drop-offs, was enough to deter most visitors, but a few dozen adventurous souls were willing to brave the hardship to witness the extraordinary scenery firsthand. The first hotel in Yosemite Valley opened for business in 1857, followed by an even larger hotel two years later. Both structures consisted of dirt floors, rooms separated by hanging sheets, and windows with no panes. But by all accounts the hospitality made up for the rustic accommodations.

Halfway along the trail to Yosemite was a large meadow called Wawona, and Galen Clark, one of the first visitors to Yosemite Valley, took up residence there in 1856. Clark built an inn for overnight guests and guided visitors to the Mariposa Grove of giant sequoias. Before long, the "Big Trees" had become a must-see destination on par with Yosemite Valley.

As news of Yosemite's extraordinary scenery rippled through California society, more and more people stopped by for a look. Artists were among the earliest arrivals, and their photos, paintings, and illustrations further fueled public curiosity. In 1861 the influential Reverend Thomas Starr King visited Yosemite Valley. Upon returning to San Francisco he preached its wonders from his pulpit and wrote compelling articles that reached a national audience.

That same year, Hutchings published *Scenes of Wonder and Curiosity in California*, an illustrated book that lavished praise upon Yosemite. To Hutchings, who would soon purchase a hotel in the Valley, Yosemite was an underexploited scenic gold mine. But as hoteliers and settlers snatched up plots of land, some visitors grew concerned at the pace of unchecked development.

Guardian of Yosemite
GALEN CLARK

In 1855 Galen Clark visited Yosemite Valley as a member of the second tourist party. Several months later he developed serious lung problems, and he was told he only had a short time to live. In 1857 Clark, who was then 42, moved to present-day Wawona. "I went to the mountains," he wrote, "to take my chances of dying or growing better which I thought were about even." Shortly thereafter, he completely recovered, and Clark spent most of his next 53 years in living in Yosemite.

Born in Dublin, New Hampshire, in 1814, Clark was a polite, sickly child who attained little success as a young man. In 1853, at the age of 39, he was broke and living in New York City when he saw an exhibition displaying gold dust from the Sierra Nevada. Enchanted, he immediately set sail for California and sought work as a gold miner.

After developing lung problems, Clark claimed 160 acres in Wawona and built a small cabin in the meadow. Awed by the immense size of the nearby giant sequoias in the Mariposa Grove, Clark wasted no time publicizing the "Big Trees" in local newspapers. Before long he was hosting paying guests at his cabin and leading them on guided tours of the Mariposa Grove. The influential Thomas Starr King called Clark, "one of the best informed men, one of the very best guides, I ever met in California or any other wilderness." Another guest described him as, "handsome, thoughtful, interesting, and slovenly."

Although generally well-liked, Clark had many unusual habits. He frequently walked barefoot, claiming that shoes and boots were "cruel and silly instruments of torture, at once uncivilized, inhuman, and unnecessary." Clark also insisted on breathing through his nose while he hiked. "As the air rushes through the nostrils on its way to inflate the lungs," he explained, "the brain attracts and inhales electricity from it."

When the Yosemite Grant was created in 1864, Clark was a natural choice to become the first "Guardian of Yosemite" (a position comparable to park superintendent today). Clark later befriended John Muir and became a charter member of the Sierra Club. Muir described Clark as "the best mountaineer I ever met, and one of the kindest and most amiable of all my mountain friends."

In 1910, 53 years after coming to Yosemite to die, Galen Clark passed away at the age of 96. He was buried near Yosemite Falls at a spot he had personally selected decades earlier. His gravesite, marked by a granite tombstone, is surrounded by giant sequoia seedlings that Clark himself planted. Today, over a century later, those young sequoias continue to grow.

In early 1864, a group of influential citizens approached California Senator John Conness with a novel idea. The group believed that a location as unique as Yosemite should belong to the public, as opposed to a handful of private landowners, and they urged the creation of a state-owned land trust to preserve Yosemite for the enjoyment of future generations.

Spearheading the effort was Israel Raymond, a wealthy San Francisco businessman. Raymond sent Conness a letter urging him to transfer Yosemite and the Mariposa Grove from the federal government to the State of California "for public use and recreation." Included with the letter was a set of large-format photographs of Yosemite taken by celebrated photographer Carleton Watkins.

By 1864, nearly a decade after James Hutchings first arrived in Yosemite, fewer than 700 tourists had visited Yosemite Valley. But Conness was suitably impressed by the photographs to introduce a bill in Congress. "This bill," he announced, "proposes to make a grant of certain premises located in the Sierra Nevada mountains, in the state of California, that are for all public purposes worthless, but which constitute, perhaps, some of the greatest wonders of the world." To assure the bill's passage, Conness promised his colleagues that it would not cost the federal government a dime. Congress, preoccupied with the Civil War, passed the bill without objection.

On June 30, 1864, President Abraham Lincoln signed the bill into law, creating the Yosemite Grant. Although hardly anyone realized it at the time, the Yosemite Grant was a radical achievement unprecedented in human history. Never before had a government set aside a piece of wilderness for its citizens based solely on its natural beauty. It was an idea that would turn out to be highly contagious, not just in America but around the world.

YOSEMITE ARTISTS

Eadweard Muybridge

Eadweard Muybridge was not the first photographer to visit Yosemite, but he was the first photographer to take a romantic approach, composing his shots like landscape paintings and adding embellished details like clouds as he saw fit. Following his first visit to Yosemite, Muybridge (who had a flair for drama) secretly adopted the pseudonym "Helios." He then exhibited Helios' Yosemite photographs in a San Francisco gallery and handed out brochures commenting on the "anonymous" artist's supreme talents. The response was overwhelming: people loved the mystery photographer's painterly approach. When it was revealed that Muybridge was Helios, critics were appalled, but the public reacted with a collective shrug and Muybridge's career continued to thrive.

In 1871, at the age of 41, Muybridge married his 21-year-old photography assistant. A few years later, convinced his wife was cheating on him, Muybridge tracked down her supposed lover to a home near Calistoga and shot him through the heart. He then apologized to several women present, calmly sat down in the parlor, and began reading a newspaper. He was ultimately acquitted of the murder on the grounds of "justifiable homicide." Later Muybridge abandoned landscape photography to focus on photographic motion studies, which laid the groundwork for the invention of motion pictures a decade later.

Albert Bierstadt

Many painters visited Yosemite in the mid-1800s, but none derived as much fame or success from the scenery as Albert Bierstadt. When Bierstadt arrived in Yosemite in 1863, landscape painting exhibitions drew blockbuster crowds in major American cities, offering the public a rare glimpse of the mysterious American West that few people had the time or the money to visit. Landscape artists were treated like rock stars, and Bierstadt's massive, melodramatic landscapes were among the most popular. A master of self-promotion, he displayed his works as if they were performances: charging admission, unveiling them from behind velvet curtains, lighting them dramatically, and even recommending that viewers scan them through binoculars to heighten the visual effect.

His first monumental Yosemite painting, *Looking Down Yosemite Valley, California* (above), measured 40 square feet and was unveiled to the public in 1865. The painting established Bierstadt as America's top landscape artist, and the giant canvas promptly toured several major cities. In 1867 a wealthy financier commissioned a massive 140 square-foot Yosemite painting for the astounding sum of $25,000. When that painting, *The Domes of Yosemite*, was unveiled to the public, it caused a firestorm of criticism. Some considered it Bierstadt's finest work, but others accused Bierstadt of vulgar exaggeration. The scenery was simply too perfect. When Mark Twain viewed the canvas he joked that it was, "considerably more beautiful than the original," describing it as, "more the atmosphere of Kingdom-Come than of California." Although some critics scoffed, Bierstadt remained one of the most popular and influential landscape artists of the 19th century.

JOHN MUIR

Of all the great artists and thinkers that Yosemite has nurtured, none has been more celebrated, more influential, and more romanticized than John Muir. His eloquent nature writing helped inspire the modern environmental movement, and his tireless efforts were vital to the establishment of Yosemite National Park.

Born in Scotland in 1838, Muir moved to Wisconsin with his parents when he was a child. His father was a Presbyterian preacher who demanded that young John memorize the Bible word for word, which he did. Later, Muir enrolled at the University of Wisconsin, but he quit before graduation to enter what he called "the University of the Wilderness." In 1867, after recovering from a factory accident that nearly left him blind, he embarked on a 1,000 mile walk to Florida.

From Florida Muir set sail for California, arriving in San Francisco in 1868. He immediately set out on a six-week walk to Yosemite. Spellbound by Yosemite's scenery—"every feature glowing, radiating beauty that pours into our flesh and bones like heat rays from fire"—Muir found employment the following summer as a sheepherder in the Sierra Nevada. Wandering among the alpine meadows with a St. Bernard, Muir rejoiced in the mountain wilderness. In his free time he studied plants and climbed the granite peaks. "This June seems the greatest of all the months of my life," he wrote, "the most truly, divinely free." By the end of the summer, Muir had developed a passion for the Sierra Nevada, which he christened the "Range of Light."

The following summer Muir worked at a sawmill in Yosemite Valley, and for the next several years he rambled about the Sierra Nevada, meticulously studying the natural landscape and taking notes. He often wandered for days in the wilderness, carrying nothing more than a blanket, a notebook, some tea, and dry bread. Around this time Muir began writing popular nature articles for newspapers and magazines.

In 1880 Muir married the daughter of a wealthy California fruit farmer. Settling down for the first time in his life, he spent the next several years working the farm and raising two daughters.

But domestic life wore on Muir, and in 1888 his wife sold par-

"Climb the mountains and get their good tidings. Nature's peace will flow through you as the sunshine into the trees. The winds will blow their freshness into you, and the storms their energy, while cares will drop off like autumn leaves."

cels of the family estate to allow Muir to focus on his
wilderness studies. Shortly thereafter he teamed up with
the influential editor Robert Underwood Johnston to
spearhead the creation of Yosemite National Park.

In 1892 Muir co-founded the Sierra Club and
became its first president. His first book, *The Mountains
of California*, was published two years later when he was
56 years old. The book was an instant success, and several books followed that are now considered nature classics.
"Strange is it not that a tramp and vagabond should meet such a
fate," he wrote, "I never intended to write or lecture or seek fame in any way, I
now write a great deal, and am well known." In 1903 Muir embarked on a year-
long, round-the-world journey, then spent the final decade of his life fighting to
stop the damming of Hetch Hetchy Valley in Yosemite—a battle that was lost in
1913. Several months later, Muir died of pneumonia.

Although Muir is often portrayed as a contemplative mountain poet, his
younger days were characterized by brash, youthful machismo. His testosterone-
fueled exploits included fleeing avalanches in winter, riding out storms in 100-foot
trees, and generally risking life and limb. At one point he shimmied to the lip of
Yosemite Falls just to check out the view. Such death-defying exploits profoundly
influenced his writing. Whereas earlier environmental thinkers such as Emerson
and Thoreau took leisurely strolls through the woods, Muir threw himself into
nature with the physical vigor of an athlete.

Muir's eloquent, adventurous writing continues to resonate with a huge audience today. His extraordinary ability to communicate the importance of wilderness preservation has influenced generations of prominent thinkers, and his once
local celebrity has morphed into environmental superstardom. Today his cult of
personality can be seen on T-shirts, posters, and bumper stickers that read "Muir
Power to You!"

Muir's sketch of the High Sierra

BECOMING A NATIONAL PARK

YOSEMITE VALLEY WAS officially protected in 1864, but under lax state management it developed into a cluttered series of roads, hotels, cabins, and pastures for cattle. Land was tilled and irrigated to provide food for residents, and a timber mill provided wood for construction and heating.

Meanwhile sheepherders marched thousands of sheep through the mountains above Yosemite Valley to graze in the pristine meadows. In 1870 Joseph LeConte remarked that "Tuolumne Meadows are celebrated for their fine pasturage. Some twelve to fifteen thousand sheep are now pastured here."The combined munching, chomping, and trampling of the sheep left the delicate meadows in disarray. During John Muir's first summer as a sheepherder in the High Sierra, he witnessed this destruction first hand. "To let sheep trample so divinely fine a place seems barbarous," he wrote. Later he put the destruction in even sharper terms, referring to sheep as "hooved locusts."

In 1889, after nearly a decade spent away from Yosemite, Muir returned with Robert Underwood Johnson, editor of the influential *Century Magazine*. Muir was shocked by what he saw. In the Mariposa Grove, a tunnel had been carved into a giant sequoia as a spectacle to draw tourists. In Yosemite Valley, trash lay in open view and once-pristine meadows had been converted to pasture. Distraught, the two men headed for the High Sierra.

Around a campfire in Tuolumne Meadows, Muir and Johnson discussed the beauty of Yosemite and the threat that development and grazing posed. Johnson suggested that Muir, who by this point was a well-known nature writer, become the public voice of a campaign to preserve Yosemite as a national park. Although Yosemite Valley and the Mariposa Grove were officially protected by the state (on paper, at least), Muir and Johnson believed the mountains surrounding Yosemite—and notably the watershed that fed Yosemite Valley—also deserved protection. Yellowstone had become America's first national park 17 years earlier, and the men felt Yosemite deserved similar status.

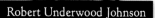

Returning from their camping trip, the two men embarked on a savvy media campaign to rally public support for their cause. Muir wrote two articles for *Century Magazine* extolling the beauty of Yosemite and the threats that it faced. In his first piece, entitled "The Treasures of the Yosemite," Muir penned some of his most enduring prose. "No temple made with hands can compare with Yosemite," he wrote, "Every rock in its walls seems to glow with life ... as if into this one mountain mansion Nature had gathered her choicest treasures."

Robert Underwood Johnson

Teddy Roosevelt & John Muir

Muir and Johnson also stumped for the creation of Yosemite National Park in speeches around the country. Their tireless efforts ultimately met with success. On October 1, 1890, Yosemite was officially designated a national park. To protect the nearly one million acres of pristine Sierra Nevada wilderness, units of the Army Calvary were dispatched to Wawona. In the summer, the Calvary patrolled the mountains on horseback, driving out sheepherders, cattlemen, and hunters.

Despite the creation of Yosemite National Park, the original Yosemite Grant, which included Yosemite Valley and the Mariposa Grove, remained under California's protection. But California was clearly not up to the task. In 1895 Muir described Yosemite Valley as "downtrodden, frowsy, and like an abandoned backwoods pasture. It looks ten times worse now than ... seven years ago. Most of the level meadow floor of the Valley is fenced with barbed and unbarbed wire and about three hundred head of horses are turned loose every night to feed and trample the flora out of existence ... As long as the management is in the hands of eight politicians appointed by the ever-changing Governor of California, there is but little hope."

Muir believed that Yosemite Valley and the Mariposa Grove needed to be permanently transferred to Yosemite National Park in order to be truly protected. That was far easier said than done. Hotel owners in Yosemite Valley vigorously opposed the idea, fearing that their businesses would be shut down if the Yosemite Grant was transferred to the federal government.

Salvation came in the form of President Theodore Roosevelt, who visited Yosemite in 1903. Although Roosevelt had specifically requested that no fanfare or celebrations herald his arrival, local residents planned a lavish banquet attended by the Governor of California and followed by an expensive fireworks display. Dismayed, Roosevelt asked Muir to show him the *real* Yosemite, and the two men quietly slipped into the backcountry for several nights of camping.

Around a roaring campfire, Roosevelt and Muir talked late into the night, slept in the brisk open air, and woke up to a dusting of snow. "I've had the time of my life," Roosevelt later told reporters. "Just think of where I was last night. Up there amid the pines and the silver firs, in the Sierran solitude, and without a tent. I passed one of the most pleasant nights of my life."

With Roosevelt's support firmly in place, Muir and the Sierra Club lobbied hard to transfer the Yosemite Grant to the National Park Service. After a bitter fight in the California legislature, the bill was passed and sent to Washington. Again Muir stepped into action, cajoling Congressmen and pulling strings to secure the necessary votes. Finally, on June 11, 1906, President Roosevelt signed the bill into law.

Elated, Muir wrote to his old friend Robert Underwood Johnson: "Sound the loud trimble and let every Yosemite tree and stream rejoice ... The fight you planned by that famous Tuolumne camp-fire seventeen years ago is at last fairly, gloriously won, every enemy down." But unknown to Muir, a new battle was looming on the horizon.

THE BATTLE FOR HETCH HETCHY

SIX WEEKS BEFORE Yosemite Valley officially became part of Yosemite National Park, San Francisco lay in ruins. On April 18, 1906, a massive earthquake shook the town, demolishing buildings and other man-made structures. Most of the damage occurred after the earthquake, however, when a massive fire raced through town and incinerated over 500 city blocks. With hopelessly limited access to water, residents could do little but watch their glorious city burn. In the end, more than half of the city's 400,000 citizens were left homeless and roughly 3,000 people died. A century later, it remains the largest loss of life due to a natural disaster in California's history.

In spite of the catastrophe, the human spirit prevailed and the citizens of San Francisco rallied to rebuild their home. It was a remarkable effort, but a vexing problem remained: San Francisco, which is situated at the tip of a small peninsula, has no natural water supply.

During the boom years of the Gold Rush, fresh water was ferried to San Francisco on schooners, poured into large casks, and hauled up the city's steep streets by weary horses and mules. (Such sorry sights inspired Andrew Hallidie, an animal lover, to invent the cable car.) Later a Roman-style aqueduct—the first in America—delivered water from a large creek 20 miles distant.

By 1906, however, this limited water supply was completely inadequate for the city's booming population—a fact that became painfully clear in the wake of the earthquake. As civic leaders struggled to build a new and improved San Francisco, one of their top priorities was securing a large, reliable source of water. And one of the most promising sites for a new reservoir was Hetch Hetchy Valley in Yosemite National Park.

Lying just 25 miles north of Yosemite Valley, Hetch Hetchy was considered by many to be Yosemite's sister valley. It too was surrounded by massive granite cliffs and thundering waterfalls, and though smaller, it was similarly impressive. The famous geologist Josiah Whitney described Hetch Hetchy as "almost an exact counterpart of the Yosemite Valley [although] not on quite as grand a scale as that valley. But if there were no Yosemite, the Hetch Hetchy would be fairly entitled to a worldwide fame."

In 1871 John Muir called Hetch Hetchy "one of Nature's rarest and most precious mountain temples." When talk of a potential dam in Hetch Hetchy first surfaced, Muir readied himself for battle. Other rivers could quench San Francisco's thirst, and Muir was determined to protect the beautiful valley where he had spent many happy days and nights. It was illegal, he pointed out, to build a dam in a national park. Dam proponents responded by introducing legislation to remove that technicality. When the legal sleight-of-hand was blocked, dam proponents presented the conflict as all of San Francisco against a few wealthy hiking enthusiasts from the Sierra Club.

Following the earthquake, Muir was up against even longer odds. The emotionally and financially shattered residents of San Francisco were desperate for peace of mind, and feasibility studies indicated that Hetch Hetchy was the most cost-effective source of water for the devastated city. Again the cry went up to dam Hetch Hetchy, but Muir and the Sierra Club fought back.

Insults were hurled back and forth, and soon the local battle spilled over into the national arena. One of the most prominent supporters of the dam was Gifford Pinchot, the brilliant young head of the U.S. Forest Service who preached conservation over preservation, so-called "wise use" that sought to sustainably protect natural resources while utilizing them for the greatest possible good. His argument for the dam at Hetch Hetchy struck a similar chord. "The injury," he wrote, "by substituting a lake for the present swampy floor of the valley ... is altogether unimportant compared with the benefits to be derived from its use as a reservoir." Visitation numbers seemed to support this—rarely did more than 200 people visit the swampy, mosquito-infested valley each summer.

Both Muir and Pinchot were devout proponents of wilderness protection, but their ideologies shared little else in common. Pinchot believed wild resources, used sustainably, should be put to the greatest possible good, while Muir, ever the romantic, wanted strict preservation for recreational use only. "Dam Hetch Hetchy! As well dam for water-tanks the people's cathedrals and churches," wrote Muir, "for no holier temple has ever been consecrated by the heart of man." It was classic Muir, wrapping nature preservation in condemnatory, religious rhetoric. In a lighter moment Muir confided to a friend, "How this business Hetch-hetchs one's time. It won't even let me sleep."

As the two sides traded barbs, the fight dragged on for many years. Using his considerable influence, Muir enlisted support from many powerful friends, including Presidents Roosevelt and Taft, who blocked any legislation favoring the dam. When Woodrow Wilson won the presidential election in 1912, however, he sided with proponents of the dam.

In less than a year, the Raker Act, which authorized the damming of Hetch Hetchy, passed both houses of Congress and was signed into law. John Raker, the bill's main proponent, claimed the reservoir would be the "highest form of conservation," making the valley more accessible and useful for recreation. "As to damning the dammers they are damned already and buried beneath a roaring flood of lies," wrote Muir, who died a year later at the age of 76.

The battle over Hetch Hetchy was a milestone in American politics. It was the first national debate to pit the necessities of urban growth against environmental preservation. As such, it set the tone for many future battles. The lessons learned by both sides were analyzed, critiqued, and refined to a high art. In the 1950s, dam builders flooded scenic Glen Canyon in southern Utah. A few years later, the Sierra Club blocked two proposed dams in Grand Canyon using a brilliant PR campaign that paraphrased John Muir. Today the ongoing debate of wise-use versus strict preservation continues to rage.

Hetch Hetchy, pre-dam

"As in Yosemite, the sublime rocks of its walls seem to glow with life, whether leaning back in repose or standing erect in thoughtful attitudes, giving welcome to storms and calms alike, their brows in the sky, their feet set in groves and gay flowers, while birds, bees, and butterflies help the river and waterfalls to stir all the air into music—things frail and fleeting and types of permanence meeting here and blending, just as they do in Yosemite, to draw her lovers into close and confiding communion."

THE NATIONAL PARK SERVICE

THROUGHOUT THE HETCH HETCHY debate, the U.S. Calvary dutifully looked after Yosemite. Although several national parks had been established by the turn of the century, the National Park Service had not yet been established, so Yosemite's operation fell to the military. After decades of exemplary service, the cavalry was replaced by a civilian force in 1914.

That same year, a wealthy industrialist named Stephen Mather wrote a letter of complaint to Secretary of the Interior Franklin K. Lane. Mather, who made his fortune mining borax in Death Valley, was frustrated with the way America's national parks were being managed, and he demanded that something be done. Lane's response: "If you don't like the way the national parks are being run, come on down to Washington and run them yourself." Mather did just that, and for the next 14 years he shaped a strong vision for America's national parks.

Mather's first step was to establish a government agency to oversee the national parks. On August 25, 1916, President Woodrow Wilson signed the Organic Act, which established the National Park Service. Mather was named director of the new agency, and his first priority was to boost park visitation. Mather realized that more visitors would translate to greater public support, which the fledgling agency desperately needed to justify its existence and ensure its future survival.

To accommodate automobiles, which were becoming increasingly popular in Yosemite, Mather secured funds to replace roads designed for horses with improved automobile roads. The result was predictable: visitation boomed. In 1915 roughly 15,000 people visited Yosemite. Five years later, that number jumped to nearly 69,000.

To accommodate the new visitors, Mather championed the construction of new hotels. "Scenery," wrote Mather, "is a hollow enjoyment to a tourist who sets out in the morning after an indigestible breakfast and a fitful sleep on an impossible bed." The park soon offered a wide range of lodging options, but the crown jewel was the sumptuous Ahwahnee Hotel—Mather's architectural masterpiece for his favorite national park.

Despite the physical improvements, many basic problems remained. Yosemite was still riddled with "inholdings" (privately owned parcels of land purchased before the creation of the park) that were vulnerable to mining, logging, and development. In 1930 John D. Rockefeller, Jr. put up half the money needed to purchase 15,000 acres of private land; the rest was provided by Congress.

Under Mather's watchful eye, Yosemite Valley became a recreational wonderland that lured thousands of tourists each year. Decades later, with annual visitation well into the millions, some would question the wisdom of this policy. But at the time, Mather's policies were essential to ensure the long-term survival of the National Park Service.

ANSEL ADAMS

Many artists have been inspired by Yosemite, but none has been as singularly identified with the park as Ansel Adams. His stunning black and white photographs elevated landscape photography to lofty new heights, and his visual genius has rarely been eclipsed.

Born to an upper-class San Francisco family, Adams was an odd, hyperactive child. A talented musician, he dreamed of becoming a concert pianist, but while recovering from an illness he discovered a copy of James Hutchings' book *In the Heart of the Sierras*. Captivated by the photographs, Adams begged his family to visit Yosemite. In 1916 his wish was fulfilled, and upon entering Yosemite Valley Ansel's loving father presented him with a fateful gift: a small Kodak camera.

At 17 Adams joined the Sierra Club and participated in many High Sierra camping trips. But he soon became frustrated with his simple camera, which took drab pictures that failed to convey the powerful emotions he felt. To remedy the situation, Adams immersed himself in advanced photography.

Over the next two decades, Adams produced hundreds of dazzling landscapes distinguished by bold, lush tonality. Assorted darkroom techniques allowed him to heighten the drama, infusing wilderness scenes with personal emotion—what he *felt* in addition to what he saw. "When I'm ready to make a photograph," he said, "I see in my mind's eye something that is not literally there ... I'm interested in expressing something which is built up from within, rather than extracted from without."

Adams' rigorous work ethic and finely-tuned creative instincts catapulted him to the top of the art world. Although his best work was done in his 20s and 30s—sometimes working at an unsustainable manic pace—in later life Adams eagerly adopted the role of elder statesmen. He campaigned on behalf of the American Wilderness and endeared himself to the public with his enthusiasm and charm. Unlike many landscape photographers, Adams was a gregarious bon vivant. He always relished a party, frequently holding forth at the piano while strong drinks were poured late into the night.

Adams served on the board of the Sierra Club for 37 years, and throughout the 20th century his wildly popular photographs inspired millions of Americans to embrace environmentalism. In 1940 his photographs helped establish Kings Canyon National Park. By 1980, when he was awarded the Presidential Medal of Freedom, he had become that rarest of breeds: an internationally famous living artist. Following his death in 1984, both the Ansel Adams Wilderness and Mount Ansel Adams in Yosemite were named in his honor.

Mount Ansel Adams

YOSEMITE ROCK STARS

BY THE DAWN of the 20th century, most famous peaks in Yosemite had been summited. A few first ascents were made by the California Geological Survey, which mapped the entire Sierra Nevada in the 1860s, but the Survey labeled several rugged peaks "inaccessible." Predictably, such declarations only whetted the appetites of hardy adventurers, and soon every notable peak in Yosemite had been conquered.

In 1931 Robert Underhill visited the Sierra Nevada and introduced mountaineering techniques from Europe. The Europeans had pioneered mountain climbing in the 1800s, and they remained the sport's preeminent practitioners for decades. Underhill helped the Americans play catch up, blazing difficult new routes up previously conquered peaks.

Following WWII and the introduction of nylon ropes, the sport of rock climbing forever changed. Prior to nylon, ropes were made out of hemp that snapped under sudden, intense pressure—a taught rope caused by a falling climber, say. As a result, falling was anathema, a fatal mistake avoided at all costs. But the new, virtually unbreakable nylon ropes allowed climbers to tackle previously unthinkable challenges. Confident that the new ropes would protect them, climbers attempted risky new moves that often caused them to fall. In the brave new post-nylon world, falling was suddenly acceptable. Through dedicated trial and error, climbers perfected complex gravity-defying moves and were soon scampering up vertical faces where no rational human belonged.

Armed with impressive new skills, climbers sought out bigger and bigger walls. And no place on Earth had more fantastically big walls in a more gloriously accessible location than Yosemite. In the 1940s and 50s, a motley collection of climbing personalities descended on the park to put their skills to the test. Among the new arrivals was a 47-year-old Swiss ironworker named John Salathé, who pioneered an important new piece of climbing equipment: the steel piton. This strong metal spike, fashioned with an eye-hole at one end, could be hammered into cracks to provide a safe, secure anchor for ropes.

Although pitons already existed in Europe, they were made with soft, malleable iron that often buckled in Yosemite's hard granite cracks. Salathé's steel pitons, by contrast, held strong and could be reused, which meant carrying much less equipment on big climbs. Salathé then unleashed another revolutionary concept in Yosemite: the multi-day climb. After climbing all day, Salathé spent the night strapped to the face of the rock. No longer constrained by equipment or daylight, climbers could rise as high as their bodies would take them.

Yosemite's pioneering "granite astronauts" soon conquered the Valley's most storied landmarks. Salathé kicked off the trend by completing the first multi-day ascent of Lost Arrow Spire (1947) and 1,500-foot Sentinel Rock (1950). In 1957 Royal Robbins, Jerry Gallwas, and Mike Sherrick climbed the vertical 2,000-foot

Lost Arrow Spire

Northwest Face of Half Dome in five days. The trio was graciously greeted at the top by Warren Harding, Robbins' rival, but the jealous Harding quickly made it his personal mission to bag the granddaddy of them all: El Capitan.

In 1958 Harding and two friends (Wayne Merry and George Whitmore) reached the top of El Capitan using "siege tactics"—setting ropes higher and higher and rappelling down for rest and supplies. It took the team 45 days spread over 18 months. Robbins considered such tactics poor form, and in 1960 he assembled a group and retraced Harding's route in a committed seven-day push.

Over the next decade, many future climbing legends came to Yosemite Valley and left their mark, establishing dozens of challenging new routes. By the early 1970s, however, the popularity of rock climbing was exploding, and the once-minimal damage caused by pitons began to raise concerns. Hammering pitons into and out of cracks distorted the rock, leaving behind a rounded scar. Many popular routes were riddled with piton marks, and the damage was compounding each year.

In 1973 three climbers—Galen Rowell, Dennis Henneck, and Doug Robinson—climbed the Northwest Face of Half Dome using radical "clean" gear that left no trace. Rather than hammering in pitons, they wedged bolt-sized pieces of aluminum into hairline cracks. The aluminum pieces were fashioned in a wide variety of shapes and sizes to accommodate whatever cracks the trio encountered, and they could easily be un-wedged without leaving a scar. *National Geographic* devoted a cover story to their endeavor, and soon chocks and nuts (as the aluminum pieces came to be called) were commercially available. A new era of rock conservation had begun. Any half decent climber could hammer their way to the top of a route, the new climbing philosophers preached, but it was better to rise to meet the challenge of the rock than to lower the difficulty of the climb to compensate for personal weakness.

Then, in the 1980s, American climbers at other popular climbing destinations began drilling many small permanent bolts into rock faces to standardize climbs. This allowed climbers to focus less on equipment and more on pure athletic ability. Although bolts were often spaced widely apart to retain the challenge of the rock, this new style of climbing, called sport climbing, met with vehement resistance in Yosemite. Purists deplored the "excessive" bolt-drilling, and many verbal—and sometimes physical—confrontations ensued. "Sport Climbing Is Neither" mocked a popular bumper sticker. Gradually, however, the practice was grudgingly accepted, and an uneasy truce has remained in place ever since.

Today roughly five percent of Yosemite visitors—nearly 200,000 people—identify themselves as rock climbers. Young climbers come to follow in the footsteps of living legends, while old timers climb well into their 60s, 70s, and even 80s. Today, as always, Yosemite Valley lies at the heart of American rock climbing. Its history, legends, and personalities have influenced several generations of climbers, and they will continue to shape the sport's culture for years to come.

YOSEMITE TODAY

TODAY YOSEMITE IS one of America's most popular national parks. Its world-class scenery lures visitors from around the globe, but the park's immense popularity now poses significant challenges. In 1855, the first year of tourism in Yosemite, 42 people visited the Valley. A century later annual visitation topped one million, and the numbers kept on climbing—two million in 1967, three million in 1987, four million in 1994. In Yosemite Valley, where most visitation is concentrated, peak-season traffic jams and long lines became as much a part of the scenery as cliffs and waterfalls. To alleviate congestion, the park service established one-way roads, initiated a free shuttle service, and reduced the number of hotel rooms and campsites.

Managing a park as large and popular as Yosemite is a complex, difficult job. The National Park Service bears the burden of both protecting the natural resources and providing for the enjoyment of park visitors—two often conflicting goals. In 2000 a general management plan outlined five main priorities for Yosemite: reduce visual intrusion of administrative and commercial services, reduce crowding, reduce traffic congestion, allow natural processes to prevail, and promote visitor understanding through enhanced interpretive programming and educational facilities. Successfully achieving these goals is a challenge. But with a dedicated staff, a passionate public following, and the support of terrific organizations like the Yosemite Conservancy, Yosemite's future looks bright.

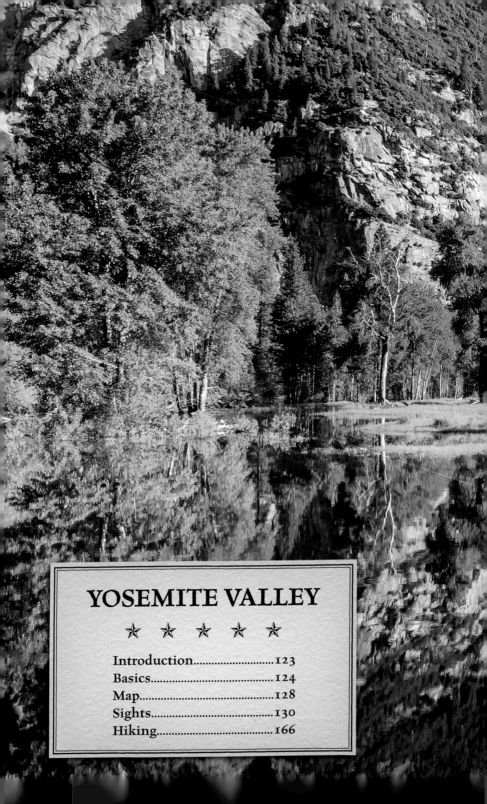

YOSEMITE VALLEY

★ ★ ★ ★ ★

YOSEMITE VALLEY

THREE THOUSAND-FOOT cliffs. Thundering waterfalls. Sparkling granite domes. Yosemite Valley is without question the most spectacular part of the park. Just seven miles long and less than one mile wide, it's home to six waterfalls over 1,000-feet tall and enough heart-pounding scenery to keep you in a perpetual state of awe. Its physical drama and picture perfect layout are almost beyond belief. As John Muir once wrote, it's "as if into this one mountain mansion Nature had gathered her choicest treasures."

First time visitors are always enchanted by Yosemite Valley. But the more you get to know it, the more enchanting it becomes. From the remarkable seasonal spectacles—the natural Firefall in late February, the spring "moonbow" of Yosemite Falls—to the sun's final rays lighting up Half Dome each evening, it seems impossible that a valley this perfect could have been created by chance. But the random, whimsical forces of geology—an upwelling of magma here, an Ice Age there—somehow conspired to produce this natural wonder. Ponder the near-impossibility of it all and Yosemite Valley becomes all the more sublime.

How you choose to bask in the Valley's beauty is entirely up to you. If you're here to relax, you can spend the day lounging along the banks of the Merced River or ride around on a narrated tour. Those looking for a bit more action can pedal along bicycle paths, hike along the Valley's stunning trails, or sign up for a rock climbing lesson. Free ranger programs are also offered throughout the day, with topics ranging from natural history to photography.

As the belle of the Yosemite ball, the Valley lures millions of visitors each year. At times, this definitely has its drawbacks. Roughly 80 percent of visitors spend their time in Yosemite Valley, and the resulting crowds sometimes create long lines and parking hassles in July and August. But no matter how crowded the Valley gets—and on popular summer weekends it can get *very* crowded—nothing can take away from the jaw-dropping scenery.

Even if you visit on busy summer weekends, there are still a few tricks to escape the crowds. Tip #1: Head to popular sights in the early morning or late afternoon—you'll avoid the worst of the crowds and enjoy the best light. Tip #2: Go for a hike—crowds thin out exponentially for every foot that you climb (hyperpopular Mist Trail notwithstanding). Even an easy stroll to Mirror Lake is capable of delivering solitude if you hike beyond the standard sights.

Yosemite Valley
BASICS

Getting Around Yosemite Valley

You can drive around Yosemite Valley, but parking is a minor hassle in spring and fall, and a big hassle in summer. My advice: park your car as soon as possible at one of the two main parking areas (see below). Then explore Yosemite Valley on foot, on bike or by riding the park's free, hybrid diesel-electric shuttle.

Yosemite's free shuttle is great if you want to explore eastern Yosemite Valley, which is home to the Valley's hotels, campgrounds and visitor facilities, plus many popular sights. In the summer two additional shuttle routes are offered. One makes quick trips between the Village Day-Use Parking Area and the Valley Visitor Center. The other heads as far west as El Capitan. (Current shuttle routes and stops are listed in the *Yosemite Guide*.) There are only two downsides to the shuttle: during peak season it often gets crowded, and it doesn't cover western Yosemite Valley, which is home to some wonderful sights.

The best way to explore Yosemite Valley is on foot or on bike, traveling at your own pace and taking plenty of time to soak in the scenery. Hikers can follow the easy 13-mile Valley Loop Trail, which circumnavigates the floor of Yosemite Valley. Bicyclists can enjoy 12 miles of traffic-free bike paths adjacent to main roads in eastern Yosemite Valley. The main paved roads are also open to bicyclists, providing access to western Yosemite Valley.

Parking

There are two major parking areas in Yosemite Valley. The largest, the Village Day-Use Parking Area, is located just south of Yosemite Village. Another large parking area is located adjacent to Curry Village.

Visitor Centers and Info

The Valley Visitor Center in Yosemite Village (p.130) is the park's main visitor center. There are also small information booths in all Yosemite Valley hotels.

Lodging & Camping

There are four hotels and four campgrounds in Yosemite Valley (p.36).

Activities
★ RANGER PROGRAMS

Free ranger programs are a great way to learn about Yosemite. Popular topics include nature, geology and photography, plus campfire and evening programs. Check the free *Yosemite Guide* for seasonal schedules.

★ BIKING

Biking is one of the best ways to explore Yosemite Valley. There are over 12 miles of paved, car-free bike paths in Yosemite Valley, and they reveal stunning scenery without the hassle of traffic and parking. You can rent bikes at Half Dome (Curry) Village and Yosemite Valley Lodge ($12/hour, $30/day).

★ RIVER RAFTING

In late spring/early summer you can float three miles down the Merced River, passing spectacular views of Yosemite Valley's sheer cliffs and thundering waterfalls. Four-person rafts can be rented at Half Dome (Curry) Village ($30/person, including a return shuttle from the river pull-out).

★ TRAM TOURS

Open-air tram tours of Yosemite Valley (two hours, $35) depart several times daily from Yosemite Lodge. Full moon Yosemite Valley tours are also offered May–October. Longer tours depart for Glacier Point. Purchase tickets at Yosemite Lodge, Curry Village or the kiosk next to the Yosemite Village Store.

YOSEMITE THEATER LIVE

These popular evening programs, held at the Valley Visitor Center from April to October, feature fascinating guest speakers. Topics include Yosemite Search and Rescue, John Muir, adventure filmmaking, and more. Tickets ($8 adults, $4 kids) are best purchased in advance at the Valley Visitor Center.

ROCK CLIMBING

The Yosemite Mountaineering School offers a wide range of climbing classes from April through October. (209-372-8344, see p.23 for more info)

Outdoor Gear/Sporting Goods
YOSEMITE MOUNTAIN SHOP

The Mountain Shop is the largest outdoor store in Yosemite, offering the best selection of hiking, camping and rock climbing gear. Located next to the Curry Village Store. Open year-round. (209-372-8396)

YOSEMITE VILLAGE SPORT SHOP

The Sport Shop offers a good selection of basic outdoor gear: boots, jackets, backpacking supplies, etc. Located next to the Village Store. Open year-round.

Dining

★MAJESTIC YOSEMITE HOTEL / AHWAHNEE DINING ROOM $$$ (Brk, Lnch, Din)

Yosemite's top dining experience features high-end California cuisine served in the Majestic Yosemite Hotel/Ahwahnee's magnificent dining hall. Locally grown ingredients are prepared with French/Italian flair. The wine list features an extensive selection of California wines. Reservations are required for dinner and recommended for other meals. Attire is "Resort Casual" (which basically means no shorts). Open year-round. (209-372-1489)

★THE MOUNTAIN ROOM $$$ (Din)

Yosemite's other top-notch restaurant offers charcuterie, steaks and sustainably harvested seafood. The wine list has a good selection of California wines. The dining hall, located at Yosemite Valley Lodge, features great views of nearby Yosemite Falls. Open year-round. (209-372-1274)

DEGNAN'S DELI & CAFE $ (Brk, Lnch)

Degnan's sells the best deli sandwiches in the Valley—perfect for a picnic lunch. A small adjacent cafe serves espresso drinks, smoothies and baked goods. Open year-round.

DEGNAN'S PIZZA LOFT $$ (Lnch on weekends, Din)

Located in the angular, 70s-chic loft above Degnan's Deli, Degnan's Pizza Loft serves—you guessed it—pizza. Salads and pasta are also available, plus cold draft beer. Arrive early to avoid long summer lines. Open spring, summer and fall.

HALF DOME / CURRY VILLAGE $$ (Brk, Lnch, Din)

Half Dome/Curry Village has multiple dining options in the spring, summer and fall. The Pavilion Buffet, located in the large building near the amphitheater, serves cafeteria-style meals at moderate prices. Nearby there's the Coffee Corner and the popular Pizza Deck. Around the corner is the Meadow Grill, which serves burgers, hot dogs and grilled sandwiches.

YOSEMITE LODGE FOOD COURT $$ (Brk, Lnch, Din)

This á la carte, cafeteria-style restaurant offers a little of everything—soups, salads, pizza, burgers, pasta, international fare. What it lacks in ambiance it makes up for in selection. Located in Yosemite Valley Lodge. Open year-round.

THE VILLAGE GRILL $ (Lnch)

This simple takeout serves burgers, fries and other fast food favorites. Located in Yosemite Village. Open spring, summer and fall.

Cocktails

THE MAJESTIC YOSEMITE HOTEL / AHWAHNEE BAR

Yosemite's most upscale bar, located in the sumptuous Majestic Yosemite Hotel / Ahwahnee (p.162), serves draft beer, wine, cocktails and tasty appetizers. You can drink inside or soak in the splendor of Yosemite Valley on the outdoor terrace. Open year-round.

THE MOUNTAIN ROOM LOUNGE

Located at Yosemite Valley Lodge, the Mountain Room is Yosemite Valley's liveliest bar, luring a steady stream of rock climbers from nearby Camp 4 (p.136). Even if you don't climb (or drink), the Mountain Room's impressive collection of vintage Glen Denny climbing photos from the 1960s are worth checking out. When the weather gets cold, the fireplace is divine. Beer, wine, cocktails and light appetizers are available. Open year-round.

PAVILION BAR

This tiny bar, located next to the Pizza Deck in Half Dome/Curry Village, serves a handful of draft beers and cocktails. Open spring, summer and fall.

Special Events

BRACEBRIDGE DINNER

Half multi-course Christmas feast, half theater-in-the-round, Bracebridge Dinner is the Majestic Yosemite Hotel/Ahwahnee's most famous tradition. Every December since 1927 this Renaissance-style dinner has featured a cast of over 100 richly costumed performers singing, dancing and serving food. Based loosely on Washington Irving's classic account of an Old English feast, Bracebridge is popular, expensive and worth it. (bracebridgedinners.com, 801-559-5000)

VINTNERS' HOLIDAYS

In November and December the Majestic Yosemite Hotel/Ahwahnee hosts several multi-day wine tastings, featuring rare and limited release wines from a number of California vineyards. Packages for Vintners' Holidays include hotel reservations, wine seminars, a Meet the Vintners Reception, and a gourmet multi-course meal at the Ahwahnee. (801-559-4884, travelyosemite.com)

CHEFS' HOLIDAYS

Held in January and February at the Majestic Yosemite Hotel/Ahwahnee, these multi-day packages cater specifically to foodies. Top chefs from around the country offer cooking classes, demonstrations, a behind-the-scenes kitchen tour, and a five-course gala dinner with paired wines. (801-559-4884, travelyosemite.com)

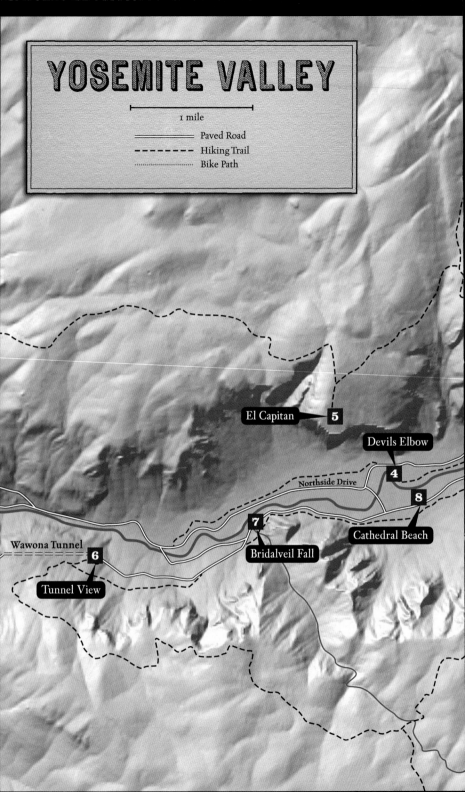

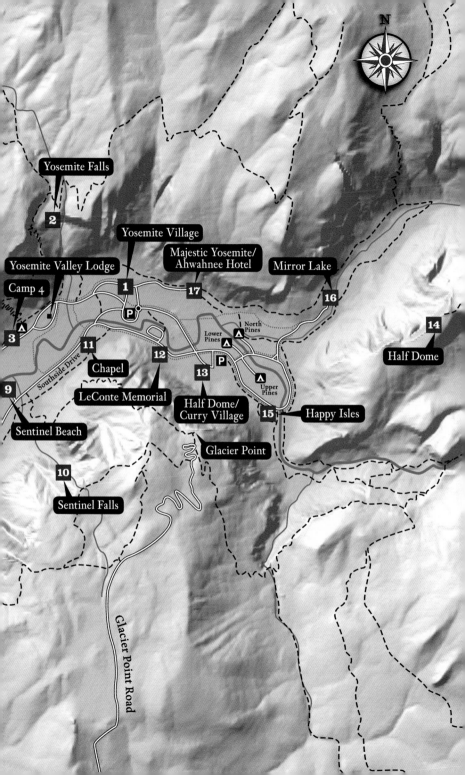

N

Yosemite Falls

2

Yosemite Village

Majestic Yosemite/
Ahwahnee Hotel

Mirror Lake

Yosemite Valley Lodge

Camp 4

1

17

16

3

North
Pines

14

Lower
Pines

Half Dome

11

Chapel

12

13

Upper
Pines

Southside Drive

LeConte Memorial

Half Dome/
Curry Village

9

15

Happy Isles

Sentinel Beach

Glacier Point

10

Sentinel Falls

Glacier Point Road

■ 1 YOSEMITE VILLAGE

❶ VISITOR CENTER

Start your Yosemite adventure at the park's largest visitor center. Inside there's a ranger-staffed help desk, a bookstore, and a large exhibit covering the history of Yosemite from geologic times to the present day. A short film, *Spirit of Yosemite*, is also shown free every half hour, and nightly performances are offered at the Yosemite Theatre from May–September. Check the *Yosemite Guide* for current Yosemite Theatre offerings.

❷ YOSEMITE MUSEUM

This small museum displays beautiful baskets and crafts from local tribes, plus exhibits on early pioneer life in Yosemite Valley.

❸ INDIAN VILLAGE

This outdoor reconstruction of a traditional Ahwahneechee village, located behind the Yosemite Museum, offers a glimpse into Yosemite Valley's native history. The self-guided tour passes by cedar-bark houses and displays on native plants.

❹ YOSEMITE CEMETERY

This is the final resting place of some of Yosemite Valley's most famous early residents, including James Hutchings (p.97) and Galen Clark (p.98), whose grave is surrounded by several young giant sequoias. A guide to the Yosemite Cemetery is available at the Visitor Center.

❺ ANSEL ADAMS GALLERY

This gallery/store features photographs, books, posters and more from Yosemite's iconic photographer (p.113). Rotating exhibits also feature the work of contemporary artists. There's a good selection of camera supplies, and photography classes (some paid, some free) are offered.

❻ WILDERNESS CENTER

If you're planning on backpacking in Yosemite, you'll want to stop here to pick up wilderness permits (p.18) and inquire about current trail conditions. The Wilderness Center also offers a good selection of backpacking-specific books, plus bear canister rentals.

❼ POST OFFICE

Want to send mom a postcard stamped "Yosemite National Park, CA 95389"? This is the place to go. Open Mon–Sat.

1 Visitor Center
3 Indian Village
2 Yosemite Museum
4 Yosemite Cemetery
5 Ansel Adams Gallery
6 Wilderness Center
7 Post Office
8 Degnan's Deli & Pizza Loft
9 Medical & Dental Center

NPS Headquarters

Village Store 10
Village Grill
Sport Shop 11

30 Min Parking
P

Village Garage

12 Yosemite Art Center

DNC Offices

← To Yosemite Lodge

To Curry Village ←

Day Parking
P

1 From Curry Village ←

1 2 4 **SHUTTLE**
5 9 10 **BUS STOPS**

8 DEGNAN'S DELI & PIZZA LOFT
Best deli sandwiches and pizza in the Valley (p.126).

9 MEDICAL & DENTAL CENTER
Hopefully you won't end up here.

10 VILLAGE STORE
This is the largest store in Yosemite Valley, and it sells just about everything: fresh food, packaged food, beer, wine, T-shirts, books, DVDs, etc.

11 SPORT SHOP
This store offers a good selection of outdoor gear, books and other supplies.

12 YOSEMITE ART CENTER
The Yosemite Art Center offers mid-day art workshops Tues–Sat during peak season. Check the *Yosemite Guide* for current offerings.

2 Yosemite Falls

This 2,425-foot, three-tiered waterfall is one of the park's most spectacular sights. If all three tiers are taken together, Yosemite Falls is the highest waterfall in North America and the fifth-highest in the world. (Angel Falls in Venezuela is the world's highest waterfall at 3,212 feet.) Individually the three tiers form Upper Fall (1,430 feet), middle cascade (675 feet) and Lower Fall (320 feet). The Ahwahneechee called this waterfall *Choo-Look* ("The Fall").

To see Yosemite Falls in its full glory, timing is key. The waterfall drains roughly 40 square miles, and its flow depends almost entirely on snowmelt. Yosemite Falls generally reaches its peak in May, when it can gush roughly 100 cubic feet per second—enough to fill a football stadium in less than a day. By mid-summer it slows to a trickle, and by autumn the waterfall is completely dry. In winter, frozen mist and fallen ice often form a 100- to 200-foot "snow cone" at the base of Upper Yosemite Falls. Another natural phenomenon, the rainbow-like "moonbow," appears in the mist during full moon nights in April and May.

Although there's a direct path to Lower Yosemite Falls from the Yosemite Falls Shuttle Stop (#6), it's much better to follow the paved trail west (left) past the restrooms and picnic tables. Soon you'll reach a spectacular path that approaches the waterfall head-on. As you walk down the path, all three tiers of Yosemite Falls are perfectly framed by towering pine trees, creating one of the most magnificent views in the park.

Follow the path until you reach a 3D bronze relief map of Yosemite Falls. Take a good look at the map and notice the hiking trail (p.182) that heads to the top of Yosemite Falls. Several hundred thousand years ago, Yosemite Falls tumbled down the upper reaches of this trail. Back then, the stream followed a channel west of its present course. Then, around 130,000 years ago, a melting glacier deposited a large pile of debris in the ancient streambed, blocking the stream, diverting it along its present course, and creating Yosemite Falls.

Continue past the 3D map until a break in the trees reveals the top of the falls. To the right of the falls you can see Lost Arrow, a towering stone pinnacle that branches off the main cliff. The name Lost Arrow comes from an Ahwahneechee legend about a hunter celebrating his conquest in the High Sierra. The hunter shot an arrow in the air, and when it landed in Yosemite Valley the arrow turned to stone. Lost Arrow was the first "big wall" rock climb attempted in Yosemite Valley. In 1947 Anton Nelson and John Salathé spent five days climbing Lost Arrow—the first time anyone had spent more than a single night on a rock face.

Continue uphill to the wooden bridge in front of Lower Yosemite Falls. If you're here in the spring, when the waterfall is at its peak, you'll be soaked in a cool spray as you cross the bridge. But be careful! The Ahwahneechee believed that a group of dangerous spirit women called *Po'-loti* lived in the waters below Yosemite Falls.

Yosemite Falls

Black Oaks

Yosemite Valley's black oaks were the Ahwahneechee Indians' most important source of food, often yielding several tons of acorns each fall. A multi-day feast accompanied the annual harvest, but most of the acorns were stored for winter use. Acorn flour was cooked into soup, mush, or bread, and the acorns from black oaks were said to be the tastiest acorns in California.

3 Camp 4

At first glance this grungy, crowded cluster of tents seems like a campsite of last resort. But Camp 4 is one of rock climbing's holiest temples—a global mecca on par with base camp at Mt. Everest. The story began in the 1950s, when pioneering rock climbers came to Yosemite to conquer the park's famous walls. Scraping out a meager existence in Camp 4, they spent years honing the culture and craft of modern rock climbing, pioneering techniques that would ultimately be used around the world. By day these "granite astronauts" climbed big walls; by night they discussed their exploits around roaring campfires. Over the years, as the popularity of rock climbing grew, Camp 4 developed a reputation as Yosemite's Climber's Camp. (Around this time a scraggly climber named Yvon Chounard began selling homemade climbing equipment in Camp 4's parking lot. He would later go on to found the outdoor clothing company Patagonia.)

In January 1997, the "Flood of the Century" washed out many of Yosemite Valley's low-lying buildings and campsites. In response, the National Park Service decided to shut down Camp 4, which lay above the floodplain, and replace it with rebuilt employee and guest housing. Upon hearing the news, a group of climbers united to save the fabled campsite. Understanding the unique role the campground had played in the global history of rock climbing, they met with park service officials to plead their case. Climbers from around the world flooded the park service with letters and phone calls attesting to the importance of the site. Suddenly aware of Camp 4's unique heritage, the park service agreed to keep the campsite open. In 2003 it was listed on the National Register of Historic Places.

Camp 4 has been called both "tent ghetto" and "home of the gods" by rock climbers—a fact that speaks volumes about the grungy, tribal culture of the sport. For many, Camp 4 is as much about socializing as actual climbing. It's where members of a scattered, global subculture go to meet, greet, see, and be seen. Friendships are made, gossip is swapped, rivalries are born, and life goes on pretty much as it always has since climbers made Camp 4 their unofficial home away from home.

4 Devils Elbow

Gloriously situated beneath El Capitan, this sandy bend in the Merced River is the perfect place to lounge around and watch the hours drift by. Located about 1.5 miles past Camp 4, Devils Elbow is best in mid- to late-summer when the water level of the Merced has dropped. While you're lounging on the banks of the river, take a look at the dark splotch on the eastern face of El Capitan. Because the splotch bears a faint resemblance to North America, this section of El Capitan is called the North American Wall.

Devils Elbow

The Ahwahneechee Legend of Tutokanula

Long ago, two bear cubs wandered away from their mother and fell asleep on a rock near the Merced River. As they slept, the rock rose high into the sky, and the cubs became stranded. All of the forest animals tried to climb the cliff to rescue the cubs, but no one—not fox, not coyote, not mountain lion—could reach the top. Finally a tiny inchworm called Tutoka offered his help. At first the other animals laughed, but Tutoka slowly made his way up the cliff. As the inchworm climbed, he chanted "Tu-tok ... Tu-tok ... Tu-tok-a-nu-la!" Upon reaching the top, the inchworm guided the two cubs down to safety.

5 El Capitan

This imposing granite monolith, rising 3,593 feet above the Valley floor, is the world's largest chunk of exposed, unbroken granite. Considered the "Crown Jewel of American Rock Climbing," it attracts thousands of climbers from around the world. During peak climbing season in spring and fall, El Capitan's sheer cliffs are covered with dozens of rock climbers. All told, there are over 70 routes to the top. A pullout on the road in front of El Capitan is a great place to look for climbers during the day, and after sundown you can often see climbers' headlamps twinkling thousands of feet above.

On average, it takes climbers four to six days to reach the top. All food, water and supplies must be hauled up the cliff by the climbers. The general rule is one gallon of water per day, which means climbers need 50 pounds of water for a six-day climb. After climbing for hours, climbers spend the night on a "port-a-ledge," a collapsible platform strapped to the face of the rock. In addition to the physical, technical and mental difficulties of climbing, all solid human waste must be collected and carried off the cliff. For years climbers brought along homemade "poop tubes" made from sawed-off sections of PVC pipe. Today specialty sanitary bags are the disposal method of choice.

The first climber to conquer El Captain was Warren Harding, who pioneered The Nose route with two friends in 1958. Using "siege tactics" (setting fixed ropes higher and higher and rappelling down for rest and supplies), it took the team 45 days spread over 18 months to reach the top. Royal Robbins, Harding's rival, considered such tactics poor form, and in 1960 he assembled a team that climbed The Nose in a self-contained, seven-day ascent. In 1975 Jim Bridwell led a team on the first one-day ascent of The Nose. And in 1993 female rock climber Lynn Hill became the first person to free-climb The Nose. (In free-climbing ropes and gear are used only for protection.) The following year Hill returned and free-climbed The Nose in a single day.

Today the current obsession is speed. In 2017, Brad Gobright and Jim Reynolds scaled The Nose in 2 hours, 19 minutes and 44 seconds. This was four minutes faster than the previous record set by Hans Florine and Alex Honnold in 2012. Some climbers have even climbed El Capitan, the northwest face of Half Dome, and El Capitan again in a *single day*. But such daring exploits are not without risk. Since 1958 over two dozen rock climbers have died on El Capitan.

Although most people dream about climbing up El Capitan, a few are obsessed with jumping off of it. The first successful BASE jump occurred in 1966, but the sport was officially banned in 1980. In 1999 a jumper drowned in the Merced River while trying to elude park rangers after an illegal jump off El Capitan. In response, a group of BASE jumpers organized a "protest" jump to showcase the safety of the sport. As spectators watched from below, a 58-year-old woman jumped off the top of El Capitan. Her parachute failed to open, and she died upon impact.

The Nose

Freerider

Dawn Wall

El Capitan

Rock Climbing El Capitan

El Capitan is the world's premier rock climbing destination, and there are over 70 named routes on the wall. The most popular is The Nose, which offers the shortest, most direct route to the top. The Nose was first climbed in 1958 over multiple days, but speed climbers now complete it in under three hours. In 2015 Tommy Caldwell and Kevin Jorgeson took 19 days to free-climb the smooth granite on Dawn Wall—considered the hardest, longest free climb in the world. Two years later, Adam Ondra completed Dawn Wall in under eight days. On June 3, 2017, Alex Honnold became the first human to climb El Capitan using no ropes or safety equipment at all, scaling Freerider in under four hours. Three days later, Leah Pappajohn and Jonathan Fleury completed the first naked ascent of El Capitan via The Nose.

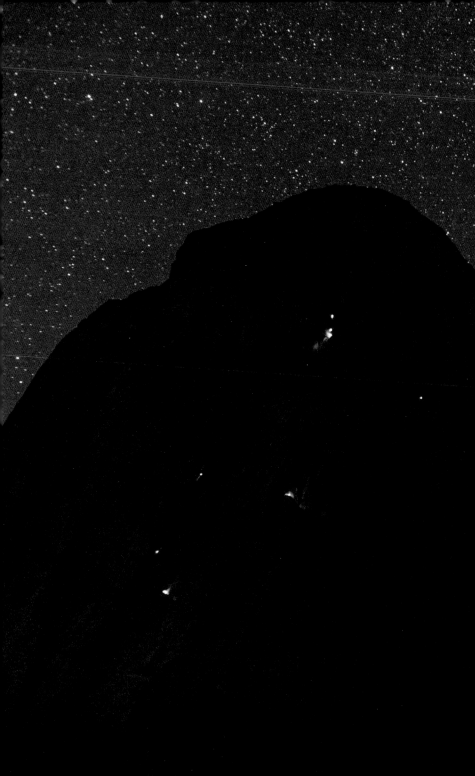

Climbers lights on El Capitan at night

"The modicum of moonlight that fell into this awful gorge gave to that precipice a vagueness of outline, an indefinite vastness, a ghostly and weird spirituality. Had the mountain spoken to me in audible voice ... I should hardly have been surprised."

—Horace Greeley, 1859

6 Tunnel View

This stunning viewpoint is one of Yosemite's must-see destinations. Perched high above Yosemite Valley's western entrance, many of the park's most notable landmarks—Bridalveil Fall, El Capitan, Half Dome—are spread out in a picture perfect display. The sweeping panorama was immortalized by Ansel Adams in his iconic 1935 photograph *Clearing Winter Storm*, which depicted the scene in the wake of a snowstorm. These days the small parking area at Tunnel View is often swarming with tourists and tour buses during the busy summer months. If you're thirsting for peace and quiet, follow the steep trail that starts in the adjacent parking area and heads to Old Inspiration Point (the original viewpoint along the old wagon road that the modern highway replaced). Follow the trail for several hundred yards and you'll be treated to equally dramatic views of Yosemite Valley high above the crowds.

Looking out over Yosemite Valley, the landscape seems eternal. But the present view is far different from the one enjoyed by early tourists in the 1850s. Prior to the arrival of Europeans, Yosemite Valley had larger meadows and open forests with trees spaced widely apart—the result of small, regular fires set by the Ahwahneechee Indians. Mature trees survived the small fires due to thick bark, but unwanted vegetation—saplings encroaching upon meadows, shrubs and debris on the forest floor—were cleared out, creating open spaces that made travel and hunting much easier. Such landscapes also favored the animals that the Ahwahneechee liked to hunt. Far from being untouched, Yosemite Valley was actively "gardened" by the Ahwahneechee. Then, throughout much of the 20th century, the National Park Service followed a policy of fire suppression to "preserve" Yosemite Valley, which inadvertently led to smaller meadows and overgrown forests. Today the park service sets intentional, small fires to help return Yosemite to its "natural" state. (See p.64 for more about fire in Yosemite.)

"The grandeur of the scene was softened by the haze that hung over the valley—light as gossamer—and by the clouds which partially dimmed the higher cliffs and mountains. This obscurity of vision but increased the awe with which I beheld it, and as I looked, a peculiar exalted sensation seemed to fill my whole being, and I found my eyes in tears with emotion."

—Dr. Lafayette Bunnell, 1851

7 Bridalveil Fall

This elegant, 620-foot waterfall is one of Yosemite Valley's most popular sights. Frequent gusts of wind often fan out the waterfall's lower curtain, giving it the appearance of a white, lacy veil—a phenomenon that inspired early explorers to name it Bridalveil. The Ahwahneechee called the waterfall *Pohono* ("Spirit of the Puffing Wind"). Bridalveil Fall is most dramatic between April and June, when melting snow creates peak runoff. During this time, a late afternoon rainbow can often be seen from the parking area, and a *double* rainbow can sometimes be seen near the base of the falls, reached via a quarter-mile path from the parking area.

Bridalveil Fall is a textbook example of a "hanging valley." Prior to the Ice Age, the Sierra Nevada was characterized by V-shaped valleys carved by rivers over millions of years. Back then, Bridalveil Creek cascaded down into the V-shaped Merced River Canyon. But when Ice Age glaciers flowed through Yosemite Valley, they gouged out the Merced River Canyon, creating a U-shaped valley with steep cliffs. When the glaciers melted, Bridalveil Creek tumbled over the edge of a cliff, creating Bridalveil Fall.

Bridalveil Fall drains roughly 20 square miles, which is half the size of Yosemite Falls' watershed. But Bridalveil Fall is often flowing in autumn long after Yosemite Falls has dried up. What's going on? Although Bridalveil Fall drains a smaller watershed, it was never scraped bare by Ice Age glaciers, and it has far deeper soil as a result. The deep soil retains more moisture, which prolongs the flow of Bridalveil Creek through the summer and into autumn.

Cathedral Spires

8 Cathedral Beach Picnic Area

This shady picnic area, nestled among ponderosa pines and incense cedars, offers great swimming in the summer along a sandy section of the Merced River. The riverbank offers tremendous views of El Capitan's southwest face, and on the opposite side of the Valley are Cathedral Spires, a pair of rock pinnacles rising 1,900 feet above the Valley floor (left). To the east of El Capitan lies Three Brothers (above), an unusual three-tiered rock formation formed by parallel faulting, which is a fancy way of saying that the rock eroded along three major sets of diagonal cracks. In 1987 a massive rockfall sent 1.5 *million tons* of granite tumbling down from Three Brothers, leveling trees and tossing giant boulders into the Merced River hundreds of yards away. The Indian name for the humped rock formation was *Kom-po-pai-zes*, which early explorer Dr. Lafayette Bunnell recorded as "mountains playing leapfrog." This was not the actual translation, however, for Bunnell admitted that "a literal translation is not desirable." Had Bunnell been less inclined towards G-rated prose, he would have translated *Kom-po-pai-zes* as ... umm ... "a couple engaged in an act of passion."

9 Sentinel Beach Picnic Area

This picnic area is similar to Cathedral Picnic Area, with picnic tables and a restroom nestled among a shady grove of trees. This is also the stopping point for Merced river rafters (p.125).

10 Sentinel Falls

This classic "stairstep" waterfall tumbles down a series of gorgeous mini waterfalls, which, if added together, measure 2,000 feet, making Sentinel Falls the second-highest waterfall in Yosemite Valley after Yosemite Falls (2,425 feet). By volume, however, Sentinel Falls is rather small, which means you'll have to visit in the spring or early summer to catch a glimpse of its beauty. Although the waterfall generally dries up by mid-summer, towering Sentinel Rock stands guard to the left year-round. According to early California geologist Josiah Whitney, 7,038-foot Sentinel Rock was named for its "fancied likeness to a gigantic watch-tower."

11 Yosemite Chapel

Built in 1879, this quaint little chapel is the oldest building in Yosemite Valley still in use today. Graced with stunning views of Yosemite Falls and the surrounding cliffs, the chapel is popular for weddings, marriage vow renewals, baptisms, and other special occasions (yosemitevalleychapel.org). Non-denominational services are open to the public every Sunday at 9:15 am, with a second service held at 11 am from Labor Day through Memorial Day.

Sentinel Fa

12 LeConte Memorial

This charming granite building, built in 1903, is the home of the Sierra Club in Yosemite Valley. It was named for Dr. Joseph LeConte, one of the first professors at the University of California, Berkeley and a co-founder of the Sierra Club. LeConte was a geologist who was known for his eloquent writing. In *A Journal of Ramblings Through the High Sierras of California* he wrote, "Was there ever so venerable, majestic, and eloquent a minister of natural religion as the grand old Half Dome?" Not surprisingly, he became good friends with John Muir, and LeConte helped Muir found the Sierra Club in 1892.

In 1901 LeConte died of a heart attack in Yosemite Valley. Shortly thereafter, a group of friends, professors, and former students donated money to construct a building in his honor. Originally constructed in Curry Village, LeConte Memorial was moved to its present location in 1919. For years it served as the main visitor center in Yosemite Valley, and between 1920 and 1923 Ansel Adams served as the building's caretaker. Inside you'll find exhibits about the history of the Sierra Club and a library filled with nature books. The building is open Wed–Sun, 10am–4pm, May–September. Free evening programs are also offered on weekends.

Joseph LeConte

13 Half Dome Village (Curry Village)

This dense cluster of tent cabins, shower houses, shops and restaurants throbs with activity in spring, summer and fall. Along with Yosemite Village, Half Dome Village (previously Curry Village, see page 36) is one of Yosemite Valley's two major visitor hubs.

Curry Village was established in 1899 by David and Jennie Curry. At the time, there were several hotels in Yosemite Valley, but at two dollars per night "Camp Curry" undercut them by half. Its motto: "Three squares a day, a clean napkin every meal, and NO tipping!" The couple started out with seven tent cabins, but expanded to 25 by the end of the summer. Each morning at sunrise, David Curry would bellow out, "Those who do not rise for breakfast by eight am will have to postpone it until tomorrow. At eight o'clock the cook gets *hot* and burns the breakfast!"

To entertain guests after sundown, Camp Curry offered evening programs that featured music, singing and storytelling. The most famous attraction, however, was the legendary Firefall (see following page). Today the original "Camp Curry" sign still hangs over the entrance, evening programs still entertain visitors, and over 400 tent cabins continue to offer Yosemite Valley's best budget lodging.

David Curry

Horsetail Falls

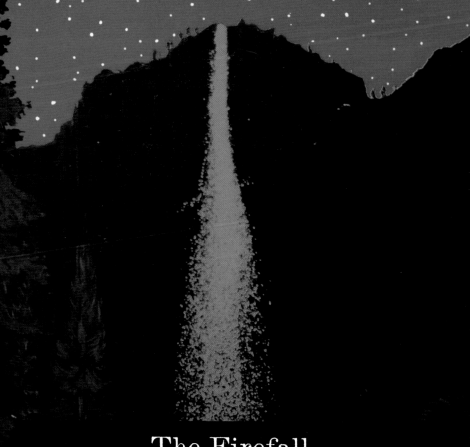

The Firefall

For nearly 100 years, from 1872 to 1968, the Firefall was one of Yosemite Valley's most popular sights. Every night in the summer, a huge pile of red-hot embers was pushed off the edge of Glacier Point, creating a glittering "waterfall" of fire that tumbled down the 3,000-foot cliff. The spectacle drew thousands of visitors to Curry Village, where the views were most spectacular. At 9pm sharp, a master of ceremonies would shout out "Let The Fire Fall!" and the embers would come tumbling down as live music played in the background.

In 1968 the park service permanently ended the Firefall, which by that point was considered artificial and unnatural. But a few years after the Glacier Point Firefall was extinguished, a "natural Firefall" became popular on the opposite side of Yosemite Valley. During the last two weeks of February, weather permitting, the final rays of the sun stream through Yosemite Valley at just the right angle to light up Horsetail Fall, which tumbles down the eastern face of El Capitan. Today the natural Firefall attracts photographers and spectators from around the world. Hotels are booked months in advance, and photographers arrive hours before sunset to stake out the perfect spot. For more on the Firefall, visit yosemitefirefall.com

14 Half Dome

Half Dome, the park's grand icon, looms over the eastern end of Yosemite Valley like a granite monarch. Rising over 4,800 feet above the Valley floor, it reaches a maximum height of 8,842 feet. From most viewpoints in the Valley, Half Dome's rounded backside and sheer eastern face make it appear exactly like half of a squat, rounded dome. But this is an optical illusion. Viewed from Washburn Point (p.193), you'll see that its rounded backside is nearly as steep as the sheer northwest face. The three dimensional map of Yosemite Valley in the visitor center (p.130) further reveals that Half Dome is actually more like an elongated ridge. Some geologists have estimated that roughly 80 percent of the original dome is still intact. If you've ever wondered what happened to the other half of Half Dome, the unsatisfying answer is: there never was another half!

But what accounts for Half Dome's sheer, 2,200-foot northwest face? When Half Dome formed millions of years ago (due to compressional forces and the erosion of previously overlying rocks), it was riddled with vertical cracks. During the Ice Age, when glaciers repeatedly flowed down Tenaya Canyon past Half Dome's northwest face, they chipped off rocks along the natural cracks. Geologists speculate, however, that the upper 500 to 900 feet of Half Dome protruded above even the highest glaciers. The upper reaches of Half Dome's northwest face, therefore, were shaped mostly by rockfalls along the vertical cracks, which were probably accelerated by the glacial removal of the supporting rocks below.

In 1868 California state geologist Josiah Whitney proclaimed that Half Dome was "probably the only one of all the prominent points about the Yosemite which never has been, and never will be, trodden by human foot." Predictably, attempts to climb it were soon underway. Although any decent hiker could reach the rounded backside of Half Dome, the final 700-foot, 45-degree ascent was simply too steep to hike.

In 1875 Yosemite Valley blacksmith George Anderson attempted to climb Half Dome by applying sticky pine pitch to the bottom of his bare feet. When that didn't work, he spent several weeks drilling iron eye-bolts into the granite. Standing on the bolts as he drilled new ones above and stringing the bolts together with rope, he soon reached the 13-acre summit. Anderson's rope-strung bolts remained the standard route for years, but they have since been replaced with a slightly more advanced metal cable system. Today thousands of hikers make the trek to the top of Half Dome each year.

In the 1950s, ambitious young rock climbers began setting their sites on Half Dome's sheer northwest face. In 1957 Royal Robbins led a team of rock climbers on the first ascent of Half Dome's northwest face. The astounding five-day climb was considered the hardest route in North America at the time. Ten years later Liz Robbins, Royal's wife, became the first woman to climb the northwest face of Half Dome.

The Ahwahneechee Legend of Tissayak

Long ago, a woman named Tissayak and her husband Nangas traveled to Yosemite Valley from the arid plains. Exhausted after the long journey, Nangas lost his temper and hit Tissayak. As Tissayak dashed up Yosemite Valley, acorns spilled out of her basket, and those acorns later grew into oak trees. When Tissayak reached Mirror Lake, she drank it dry. When the thirsty Nangas approached, he grew enraged and hit her again. As Tissayak threw her basket at Nangas, the angry gods turned the couple into stone. Nangas became North Dome (with Basket Dome above) and Tissayak became Half Dome, her tears marked by dark streaks on the vertical face. For the rest of eternity the quarreling couple must now face each other in silence.

15 Happy Isles

This leafy stretch of the Merced River, lying just east of Curry Village, is the jumping off point for the Mist Trail, the most popular hike in the park (p.166). As a result, it's almost always buzzing with activity in the summer. The name Happy Isles comes from three nearby islands in the Merced River. The road to Happy Isles is off limits to private vehicles, so visitors must walk here or take the free shuttle. A short distance from shuttle stop #16 is the family-friendly Nature Center at Happy Isles (open May–mid-Sept). This small museum is filled with natural history displays and serves as Yosemite's headquarters for the kid-oriented Junior Ranger Program.

In July 1996, Happy Isles was the site of one of Yosemite Valley's most notorious rock falls. Over 70,000 tons of rock detached from the cliffs above and went into free fall, hitting the ground at roughly 260 miles per hour. The granite pulverized instantly, generating a 250 mph blast of wind that toppled over 700 trees and sent rock fragments hurtling through the air. Remarkably only one hiker was killed. Today you can still see many of the fallen trees in the vicinity of Happy Isles.

16 Mirror Lake

Mirror Lake is a great destination for anyone looking to escape the crowds and soak in Yosemite's natural scenery. The short, easy trail starts at shuttle stop #17, crosses Tenaya Creek Bridge, and then follows Tenaya Creek up to Mirror Lake. Mirror Lake is best viewed in the spring and early summer when the water level is high. For the best reflections, walk along the east side of the lake in the morning and the west side in the late afternoon. These days Mirror Lake is more of a pond than a lake, and each year it grows smaller as more and more vegetation fills in the water. Someday in the not so distant future, Mirror Lake will become Mirror Meadow.

Mirror Lake originally formed due to the largest known rockfall in the history of Yosemite Valley. At some point in the distant past, over 15 million cubic yards of debris came crashing down from the western cliffs above, damming Tenaya Creek and creating Mirror Lake. The uphill path to Mirror Lake actually travels over the dam created by the rock avalanche.

More recently, in March, 2009, the Ahwiyah Point rockfall sent roughly 45,000 cubic meters of rock tumbling down below Half Dome. The air blast knocked down over 100 trees, and the crash was equivalent to a 2.4 earthquake as measured by nearby seismometers. The rockfall also buried a southern section of the 5-mile loop trail that circumnavigates Mirror Lake, closing that portion of the trail for over three years until workers established a new path.

Mirror Lake

17 Majestic Yosemite Hotel (Ahwahnee)

The Majestic Yosemite Hotel (formerly Ahwahnee Hotel, see page 36) is the pinnacle of luxury in Yosemite—which isn't surprising given the $460 per night price tag. The hotel's most expensive suite, which comes with a library parlor, rents for over $1,100 per night. But even non-guests can enjoy a stroll through the hotel's sumptuous interior or a meal in the grand dining room (p.126). And nothing tops off a long day of hiking like a cocktail at the hotel bar. Guided tours of the hotel are offered throughout the year (inquire at the concierge desk).

The Ahwahnee Hotel opened in 1927. Its construction was spearheaded by Stephen Mather, the first director of the National Park Service, who wanted a world-class lodge for his favorite national park. From a distance the hotel appears constructed of stone and timber, but a closer look reveals the "timber" is actually molded concrete. In the early 1900s fire destroyed several grand national park lodges, so Mather insisted the Ahwahnee be fire resistant. Although concrete supports were used, they were poured into wood-grain molds and painted to look like wood. Real timber is only found in the dining room.

Dozens of celebrities have stayed here, including Queen Elizabeth, Eleanor Roosevelt and Presidents John F. Kennedy and Barack Obama (both of whom arrived by helicopter). Lucille Ball, Desi Arnaz and Judy Garland stayed here while filming *The Long, Long Trailer*, as did William Shatner and Leonard Nimoy while filming *Star Trek IV*. Robert Redford worked at the hotel as a young man, and Steve Jobs was married on the back lawn in a Buddhist ceremony.

Ahwahnee Dining Room

The Ahwahnee's Great Lounge is famous for warm fires in the winter and tea and cookies served to guests every day at 4pm. If the room seems hauntingly familiar, there's a good reason: it was used as a model for one of the interior sets in Stanley Kubrick's 1980 film *The Shining*.

⊲ THE MIST TRAIL ⊳

SUMMARY The Mist Trail is the most popular trail in Yosemite, and with good reason. Although relatively short by Yosemite standards, it passes by some of the park's most dramatic scenery. The Mist Trail skirts the boulder-strewn banks of the Merced River, then heads up a series of stone steps in front of 317-foot Vernal Fall. In spring and early summer, the thundering waterfall soaks hikers in a drenching, rainbow-filled spray. (Beware of slippery stone steps!) The only downside: massive crowds in the summer. On busy weekends, the hyper-popular Mist Trail can feel more like a trip to the mall than the Great Outdoors. But don't let that deter you. It remains one of Yosemite's classic hikes. (Note: after reaching the top of Vernal Fall, strong hikers can continue to the top of 594-foot Nevada Fall, which adds 1.4 miles and 1,000 feet of elevation change to a round-trip hike from Happy Isles.)

TRAILHEAD The Mist Trail starts in Happy Isles (shuttle stop #16) at the far eastern end of Yosemite Valley. From the shuttle stop, cross the stone bridge and follow the well-trodden path to your left.

TRAIL INFO

DIFFICULTY Strenuous   **HIKING TIME** 3–4 hours

DISTANCE 3 miles, round-trip   **ELEVATION CHANGE** 1,000 feet

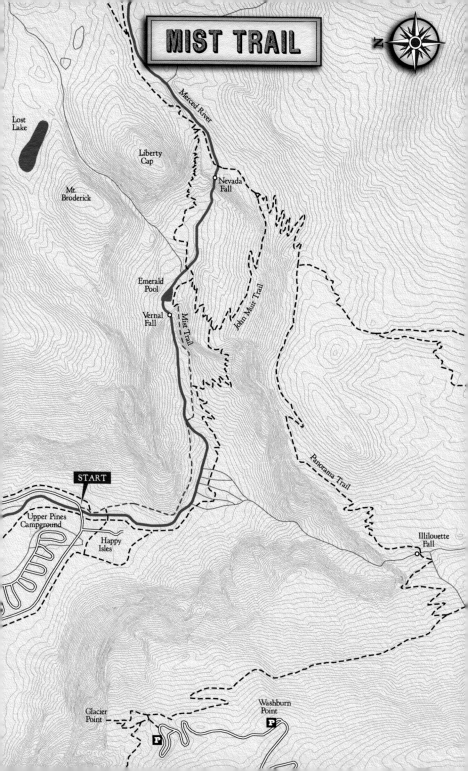

Mist Trail

"How softly these rocks are adorned, and how fine and reassuring the company they keep, their feet among beautiful groves and meadows, their brows in the sky ... bathed in floods of water, floods of light."

—John Muir

Nevada Fall

⊰ HALF DOME ⊱

SUMMARY   Half Dome is, without question, the most fabled hike in the park. This towering quirk of geology beckons every adventurer who sets eyes on it. The challenging 8.5-mile trail to the top starts in Yosemite Valley, passes by Vernal Fall and Nevada Fall, then climbs to the base of Half Dome's steep backside. From there you'll haul yourself up a pair of metal cables drilled into the rock—a vertigo-inducing experience sure to quicken any pulse. Make no mistake, this is not a trail for the faint of heart. But if you've got the physical and mental stamina to take on Half Dome, you'll be rewarded with jaw-dropping views of Yosemite Valley. It's an experience you'll never forget. Strong hikers can make it round-trip in 12 hours. If you'd like to hike Half Dome in two days, you must obtain wilderness permits to camp at Little Yosemite Valley Campground, located about halfway to the top. (See following pages for additional info.)

TRAILHEAD   The most popular route to the top of Half Dome starts in Happy Isles (shuttle stop #16) and follows the Mist Trail (p.166) to the top of Nevada Fall. From there follow the signs to the top of Half Dome.

TRAIL INFO

DIFFICULTY Very Strenuous

DISTANCE 17 miles, round-trip

HIKING TIME 12–14 hours

ELEVATION CHANGE 4,800 feet

HALF DOME INFO

Half Dome is one of America's most incredible hikes, but it's a 17-mile, 4,800-foot monster that demands respect. Advance preparation is necessary.

CABLES

The final 700-foot ascent to the top of Half Dome is inclined between 45 and 60 degrees, which is far too steep to hike. Half Dome's unique cable system (photo p.176) puts the otherwise inaccessible peak within the reach of hikers. Two sets of steel poles are set into the rock at 10-foot intervals, and metal cables are strung between the poles. The cables are set 30 inches apart—small enough to grasp a cable with both hands, but large enough for two people to squeeze past one another. Many hikers use thick work gloves to protect their hands and enhance their grip. Wooden boards are laid flat between each set of poles, offering hikers a foothold to rest along the way. The cable system is installed in the spring, then taken down in the fall to protect it from winter snowslide damage. Exact dates vary based on conditions. Check the park's website for the most up-to-date info.

ONE DAY OR TWO?

It's possible to hike Half Dome in a single day if you're an experienced hiker in great shape. But I prefer splitting up the hike over two days, giving yourself plenty of time to soak in the magnificent scenery. Overnight hikers spend the night at Little Yosemite Valley Campground, which offers the closest backcountry camping near Half Dome. Located a mile above Nevada Fall, the campground has food lockers and composting toilets, but no potable water. (There's a stream nearby.) You'll need a wilderness permit (p.18) to camp there. I like hiking to the campground on the first day, then heading up Half Dome early the next day.

CHOOSING THE BEST ROUTE

There are three popular routes to Half Dome, all of which converge at the top of Nevada Fall. The first route starts in Happy Isles and follows the Mist Trail to the top of Nevada Fall. The second route starts in Happy Isles and follows the John Muir Trail to the top of Nevada Fall. Although the Mist Trail is 1.5 miles shorter and more scenic than the John Muir Trail, the John Muir Trail has fewer crowds and a gentler grade.

The third route starts at Glacier Point and follows the Panorama Trail to the top of Nevada Fall. This route is about two miles longer than Nevada Fall via the John Muir Trail, but because it starts at a higher elevation you'll save roughly 1,100 feet of climbing. That said, the Panorama Trail drops roughly 1,500 feet as it descends to Illiloutte Falls—not bad on the way out, but a tough way to finish a long hike.

My favorite route starts at Glacier Point and finishes in Yosemite Valley. This requires catching the bus to Glacier Point (p.191) or shuttling two cars between Glacier Point and Yosemite Valley.

PERMITS

A maximum of 300 hikers (225 day hikers, 75 backpackers) are allowed on top of Half Dome each day. Permits for day hikers are distributed by lottery on recreation.gov. There is one pre-season permit lottery in March, plus daily lotteries for about 50 permits during hiking season. Backpackers should apply for Half Dome permits when they apply for wilderness permits (p.18). For comprehensive Half Dome permit info, visit the Yosemite National Park website.

WHAT'S ON TOP?

The top of Half Dome is a vast, mostly flat surface that's about the size of 17 football fields. Chipmunks and marmots are common, and the rare Mount Lyell salamander has been spotted. Over half a dozen very small trees once grew on the summit, but most were used for firewood when overnight camping was allowed on top of Half Dome. (Overnight camping was banned in 1993 due to the large amounts of human waste generated.)

DO NOT ASCEND THE CABLES IF DARK CLOUDS ARE VISIBLE!

During thunderstorms Half Dome is a giant lightening rod, and hikers on top have been killed by lightning strikes. A warning sign below the backside of Half Dome states: "DANGER. If a thunderstorm is anywhere on the horizon, do not pass beyond this sign. Lightning has struck Half Dome during every month of the year." A single bolt of lightening contains up to one hundred million volts and reaches temperatures up to 55,000 °F—five times hotter than the sun. Thunderstorms descend on Half Dome with remarkable speed, and you don't have to be on top to feel the effects. Rock climbers stranded on the sheer northwest face during thunderstorms have been shocked by lighting-induced electrical charges streaming across the wet granite. Hikers fleeing thunderstorms have been severely shocked while gripping Half Dome's metal cables.

DEATH ON HALF DOME

There have been over 20 recorded deaths on Half Dome. In 1972 a hiker on top of Half Dome took refuge from a lightning storm in a small cave. He was killed when lightning struck the cave. Thirteen years later, a group of young hikers ascended the cables during a lightning storm and sought refuge in the same cave. Lightning struck the cave again, killing one hiker and sending another into seizures that propelled him off the sheer northwest face.

Thousands of hikers use Half Dome's cables each year, but only five people have died while ascending or descending the cables. Many of these accidents occurred when the granite was slippery and wet. Other causes of death on Half Dome include suicides (6), falls while rock climbing (4), and unsuccessful BASE jumps (2).

Half Dome Cables

View from Half Dome

⊰ FOUR MILE TRAIL ⊱

SUMMARY   Millions of tourists drive to Glacier Point to check out the stunning views, but those views are even more rewarding when you've earned them via the Four Mile Trail. This is one of the best hikes in Yosemite Valley, with unrivaled views of Yosemite Falls. If hiking 3,200 feet up isn't your thing, try riding the bus to Glacier Point (p.191) and hiking 3,200 feet *down* to Yosemite Valley. Conversely, if hiking *just* 9.2 miles isn't your thing, consider the following 13.1-mile hike: head up the Four Mile Trail, then hike down the Panorama Trail to the top of Nevada Fall, then hike down to Yosemite Valley via the Mist Trail (p.166). If you've got the time and the energy, the Four Mile Trail/Panorama Trail /Mist Trail route is one of the finest hikes in the park. So why is it called the Four Mile Trail when it measures 4.6 miles long? The original trail, built in the 1870s by James McCauley, was exactly four miles long, but it has since been improved and extended.

TRAILHEAD   The Four Mile Trail starts between Sentinel Beach and Swinging Bridge on Southside Drive.

TRAIL INFO

DIFFICULTY Strenuous	**HIKING TIME** 5–7 hours
DISTANCE 9.2 miles, round-trip	**ELEVATION CHANGE** 3,200 feet

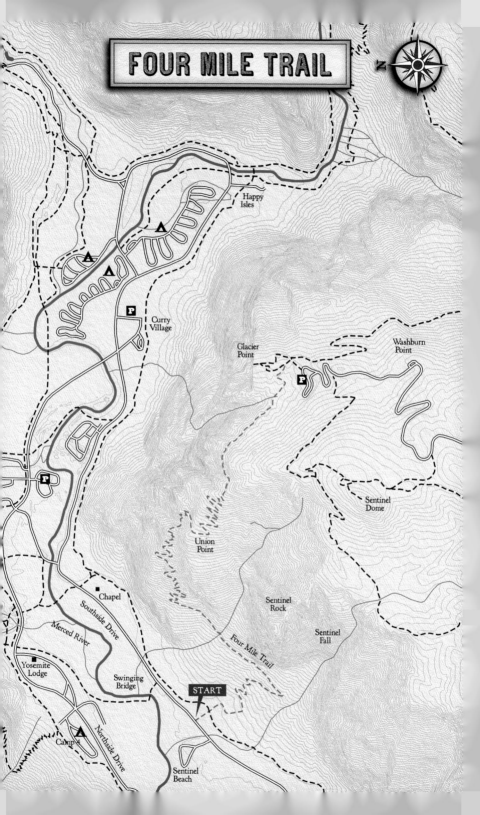

❧ YOSEMITE FALLS ❧

SUMMARY   If you love 2,400-foot waterfalls and strenuous hikes, it doesn't get better than this. You'll pant and sweat all the way to the top, but there's no better way to revel in the majesty of Yosemite Falls. After climbing the trail's 135 switchbacks, you'll be treated to sweeping views of Yosemite Valley and amazing glimpses of Upper Yosemite Fall. The top of the trail follows a notch in the cliff that brings you above the waterfall, and from there a narrow path drops down to a fenced-in ledge beside the lip of Upper Yosemite Fall. If you're afraid of heights, the fenced-in ledge is probably not for you. But if you like dramatic views, it's well worth the effort. If you don't feel like climbing all the way to the top, Columbia Point (1.2 miles from the trailhead, 1,000-foot elevation change, 80+ switchbacks) is a great destination with sweeping views of the Valley.

TRAILHEAD   The trail to the top of Yosemite Falls starts at Camp 4. Take the shuttle to Yosemite Lodge (stop #7), and cross the street to Camp 4. The hike starts between the parking area and the campground.

TRAIL INFO

DIFFICULTY Strenuous   **HIKING TIME** 4–5 hours

DISTANCE 7.6 miles, round-trip   **ELEVATION CHANGE** 2,600 feet

YOSEMITE FALLS

N

Upper
Yosemite
Fall

Middle
Yosemite
Fall

Lower
Yosemite
Fall

Columbia
Rock

Eagle
Peak

START

Yosemite
Lodge

Camp 4

Three Brothers

Northside Drive

Leidig
Meadow

Southside Drive

View from Columbia Point

"It is in no scene or scenes the chasm consists, but in the miles of scenery where cliffs of awful height and rocks of vast magnitude and of varied and exquisite coloring, are banked and fringed and draped and shadowed by the tender foliage of noble and lovely trees ... associated with the most tranquil meadows, the most playful streams, and every variety of soft and peaceful pastoral beauty."

—Frederick Law Olmstead

"Here the view is perfectly free down into the heart of the bright irised throng of comet-like streamers into which the whole ponderous volume of the fall separates, two or three hundred feet below the brow. So glorious a display of pure wildness, acting at close range while cut off from all the world beside, is terribly impressive."

—John Muir

Top of Yosemite Falls

GLACIER POINT ROAD

✶ ✶ ✶ ✶ ✶

Half Dome, Sunset

GLACIER POINT ROAD

THIS 16-MILE ROAD wraps around Yosemite Valley's south rim on its way to Glacier Point, one of the most stunning and accessible viewpoints in the park. Perched 3,200 feet above the Valley floor, Glacier Point offers jaw-dropping views of Half Dome and a panorama of Sierra spectacles: Yosemite Falls, North Dome, Clouds Rest, Tenaya Canyon, the Royal Arches. Due to its high elevation and clear skies, Glacier Point is one of the best places in California to stargaze at night. Even if you're only in Yosemite for a day, no first time visitor should leave without a visit to Glacier Point.

Most people drive to Glacier Point, revel in the scenery, then turn around and drive back. There's nothing wrong with that, but if you've got the time Glacier Point Road has some terrific day hikes. A handful of trails venture along Yosemite Valley's south rim to sweeping viewpoints, all of which are far less crowded than Glacier Point. Free ranger-led hikes are often offered (check the *Yosemite Guide* for seasonal dates and times). If you'd like to spend a day or two exploring the trails along Glacier Point Road, consider spending the night at Bridalveil Creek Campground (p.38).

Glacier Point is roughly 30 driving miles from Yosemite Valley—about an hour one-way. If you don't feel like driving, you can purchase a ticket for the four-hour Glacier Point Tour ($41 adult, $23 child, 209-372-4386), which leaves Yosemite Valley at 8am, 10am and 1:30pm from June to October. You can also ride the bus one-way to Glacier Point ($25 adult, $15 child), then hike down the Four Mile Trail (p.180) or the Panorama Trail, which heads to Nevada Fall and the Mist Trail (p.166).

In winter and early spring, most of Glacier Point Road is closed due to heavy snow, but the first six miles are plowed to Badger Pass Ski Area, a small resort with a handful of lifts. Free winter shuttles run between Yosemite Valley hotels and Badger Pass, and free ranger-led snowshoe walks are offered daily (check the *Yosemite Guide*). Cross country skiers can explore dozens of miles of nearby trails or plan an overnight trip to Glacier Point or Ostrander Lake, both of which offer overnight accommodations (p.28). Note: four-wheel drive or tire chains are required for all vehicles heading to Badger Pass in the winter.

1 Yosemite Ski & Snowboard Area

The Yosemite Ski & Snowboard Area (formerly Badger Pass, see page 36) is the oldest ski resort in California. It offers five lifts and ten runs for skiers and snowboarders. Easy terrain, short lift lines, and relatively cheap tickets make the Yosemite Ski & Snowboard Area great for families and beginners. Cross country skiers enjoy 90 miles of marked trails and 25 miles of machine-groomed track. Ski season generally runs mid-December to late March, depending on snowfall and weather conditions. A small base lodge offers food, drinks, equipment rentals and ski instruction. Weekend tickets: $47 adults, $30 kids. (209-372-1000, travelyosemite.com/winter/yosemite-ski-snowboard-area)

2 Clark Range View

This small roadside pullout offers great views of the Clark Range, one of the most rugged and remote mountain ranges in the park. In the foreground is Mt. Starr King, a conical granite dome that rises to a maximum elevation of 9,092 feet. The dome is named for Thomas Starr King, a famous Unitarian minister who visited Yosemite Valley in the 1860s and helped promote the park. Beyond Mt. Starr King is 11,522-foot Mt. Clark, the highest peak in the Clark Range. Both the peak and the range were named after Galen Clark, the first Guardian of Yosemite (p.98). Exploring the Clark Range requires several days of intense backpacking, but the reward is some of the most beautiful scenery in the park (p.210).

3 Washburn Point

This large turnout features a stunning view framed by Half Dome on the left and Mt. Starr King on the right. In the center is Merced Canyon, home to two of the park's most impressive waterfalls: Nevada Fall (594 feet) and Vernal Fall (317 feet). In the spring, when the Merced River is swollen with snowmelt, the roar of these waterfalls reaches all the way to Washburn Point.

Moments before the Merced River tumbles down Nevada Fall, the water is churned and frothed by a series of violent rapids, giving the waterfall a brilliant white color that inspired early explorers to name it Nevada (Spanish for "Snowfall"). Vernal Fall, below, was named for its "cool, vernal spray." Both waterfalls can be viewed up close along the popular Mist Trail (p.166).

The view from Washburn Point reveals that Half Dome isn't actually half of a dome. In fact, more than 70% of the dome remains intact. Half Dome's unique shape formed over millions of years due to the exfoliation of overlying rock layers. Later, during the Ice Age, glaciers chipped away its steep northwest face, giving the impression of "half a dome" from the floor of Yosemite Valley.

"[Half Dome] strikes even the most casual observer as a new revelation in mountain forms; its existence would be considered an impossibility if it were not there before us in all its reality; it is a unique thing in mountain scenery, and nothing even approaching it can be found except in the Sierra Nevada."

—Josiah Whitney

Washburn Point

4 Glacier Point

The views from 7,214-foot Glacier Point are among the most spectacular in Yosemite—and, for that matter, in America. Many of Yosemite Valley's most famous features—Half Dome, Yosemite Falls, Royal Arches, North Dome—can be seen in a single, sweeping panorama. Glacier Point is reached via a short, paved path from the large parking area. Along the way you'll pass the chalet-style Glacier Point Snack Shop and the small Geology Hut, which features diagrams detailing the geologic processes that shaped Yosemite Valley. Just below the Geology Hut is a pair of free binoculars (great for checking out the ant-like hikers on top of Half Dome) and a metal plaque that points out famous landmarks and distant peaks. Glacier Point itself is a small platform surrounded by a protective railing. Peak over the edge and you'll stare 3,214 feet straight down to the floor of Yosemite Valley.

At night, Glacier Point's high elevation, clean air, and lack of light pollution make it one of the best places in California to see the stars. Every Friday and Saturday night in the summer, rangers offer free star constellation talks, and

astronomy clubs from across California set up giant telescopes for the public to gaze into. In fact, so many astronomy clubs want to come to Glacier Point to stargaze that the park service only allows one club each weekend, and the dates are booked months in advance. If you like astronomy, a visit to Glacier Point at night is an absolute must.

As you gaze out across Glacier Point, your eyes will immediately be drawn to Half Dome, which dominates the view to the northeast. Behind Half Dome is a striking granite mountain called Clouds Rest. Although Half Dome appears higher from this perspective, Clouds Rest is actually over 1,000 feet higher. The western side of Clouds Rest, which is almost entirely bare granite, tumbles down into Tenaya Canyon. This forboding gorge has been referred to as the "Bermuda Triangle of Yosemite" because so many hikers have gotten lost there.

Until 1882 Glacier Point was only accessible via the 4-mile trail from Yosemite Valley. The trail was built by James McCauley in 1871, and for years he charged a toll of $1 per hiker. In 1878 McCauley opened The Mountain House Hotel at Glacier Point, which was later joined by the Glacier Point Hotel in 1917. Both structures burned down in 1969, however, and neither was rebuilt.

~⚘ SENTINEL DOME ⚘~

SUMMARY This short hike offers plenty of bang for your buck. At 8,122 feet, Sentinel Dome is the second highest point above the rim of Yosemite Valley (after Half Dome) and sits 1,000 feet higher than Glacier Point. Sentinel Dome's panoramic views include Half Dome, Yosemite Valley, and many distant High Sierra peaks, which can be identified using a metal plaque embedded in a boulder at the summit. Not far from the plaque is the fallen skeleton of a gnarled Jeffrey pine. This wind-contorted tree, made famous by Ansel Adams, was over 400 years old when it died during a drought in the mid-1970s. Remarkably, the skeleton remained standing until 2003. Sentinel Dome makes a fantastic sunset destination for anyone looking to escape the crowds at Glacier Point. As Dr. Joseph LeConte put it after witnessing a sunset from Sentinel Dome in 1870: "Such a sunset, combined with such a view, I never imagined."

TRAILHEAD The Sentinel Dome trail starts from Taft Point/Sentinel Dome parking area (14 miles east of Chinquapin; 7 miles west of Glacier Point). The parking area is easily identified by its open setting and small restroom.

TRAIL INFO

RATING Easy	**HIKING TIME** 1 hour
DISTANCE 2.2 miles, round-trip	**ELEVATION CHANGE** 380 feet

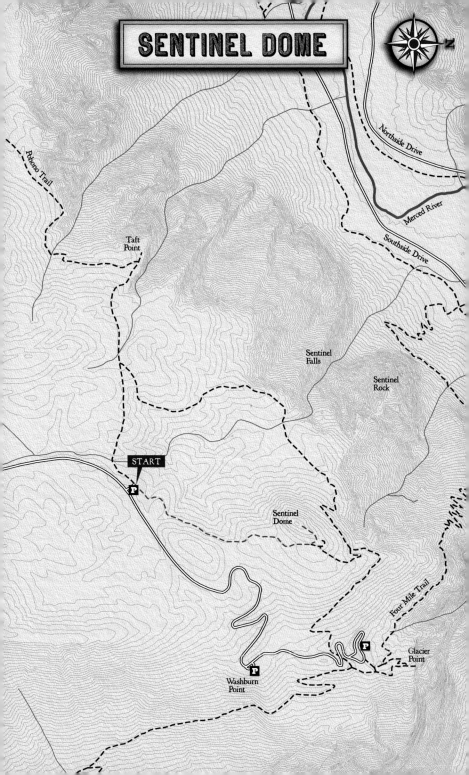

◄ TAFT POINT ►

SUMMARY This easy hike drops down and twists through some towering pines before reaching an exposed granite ledge at the edge of Yosemite Valley. A high point along the ledge marks Taft Point, a vertigo-inducing precipice that looms over Yosemite Valley. A small metal railing is all that protects you from the stomach-churning, 3,400-foot drop. Taft Point (7,503 feet) offers great views of Yosemite Falls and the Merced River twisting along the Valley Floor, but the sensational views of El Capitan are what really sets this spot apart. Also keep your eyes out for the famous Taft Point Fissures, natural cracks in the rock that plummet hundreds of feet straight down. A few of the fissures have large rocks lodged in their narrow openings. Taft Point was named for President William Taft, who visited Yosemite in 1909.

TRAILHEAD The Taft Point trail starts from Taft Point/Sentinel Dome parking area (14 miles east of Chinquapin; 2 miles west of Glacier Point). The parking area is easily noticed by its open setting and small restroom.

TRAIL INFO

RATING Easy

HIKING TIME 1 hour

DISTANCE 2.2 miles, round-trip

ELEVATION CHANGE 250 feet

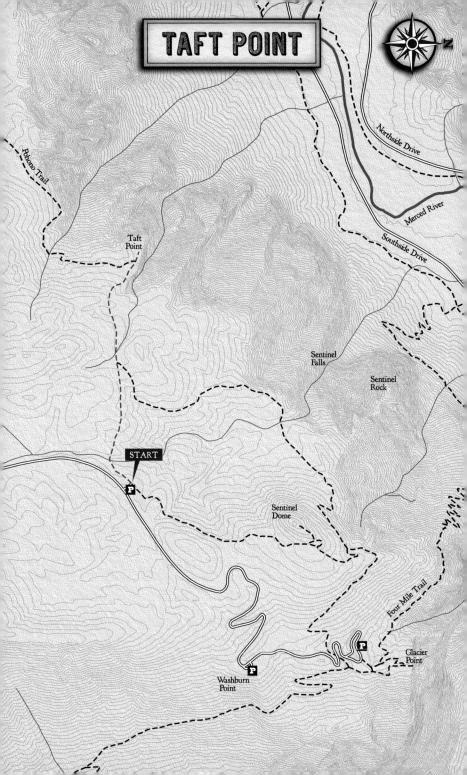

⮌ OSTRANDER LAKE ⮌

SUMMARY   Most hikers who visit Glacier Point Road gravitate to trails along the rim that offer spectacular views of Yosemite Valley. But this beautiful lake, nestled among sparkling granite slopes, is a terrific destination if you're afraid of heights or enamored with pristine alpine lakes. From the trailhead you'll pass through 2.5 miles of relatively flat terrain. Bear left at the first trail junction (1.4 miles), then left again at the second (2.7 miles). Next, prepare yourself for the trail's most difficult stretch: a 1,500-foot vertical ascent. Towards the top of the climb you'll skirt Horizon Ridge, which offers terrific views of Mount Starr King and the Illilouette Creek Basin. After peaking at 8,720 feet, the trails drops down 200 feet to Ostrander Lake. On the lake's northern shore you'll see Ostrander Ski Hut, a rustic stone building where crosscountry skiers can spend the night in the winter (p.28).

TRAILHEAD   The Ostrander Lake trailhead starts from the Ostrander Lake parking area (9 miles east of Chinquapin; 7 miles south of Glacier Point). Restrooms are available at the parking area.

TRAIL INFO

RATING Moderate	**HIKING TIME** 6–8 Hours
DISTANCE 11.4 miles, round-trip	**ELEVATION CHANGE** 1,720 feet

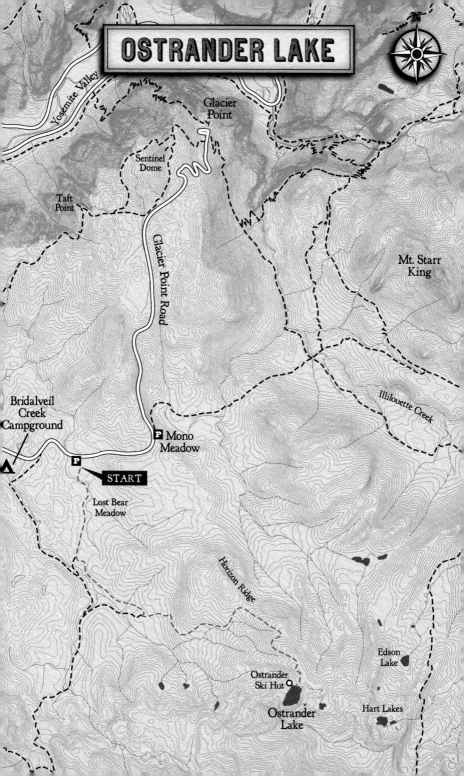

~ POHONO TRAIL ~

SUMMARY   On busy weekends when Yosemite gets crowded and congested, the Pohono trail offers hikers a well-earned sense of solitude. Despite its breathtaking views of Bridalveil Fall, Ribbon Fall, and El Capitan, the Pohono Trail remains relatively uncrowded. While other tourists are trying to find a parking space, you can soak in the Valley's majesty high above it all. Whether you're day hiking or backpacking, the Pohono Trail never disappoints. Although the complete 13.8-mile Pohono Trail stretches from Tunnel View (p.144) to Taft Point (p.202), you can reach the most spectacular viewpoints—Dewey Point (above), Crocker Point, Stanford Point—via a hike from Glacier Point Road. The hiking distance listed below is for a round-trip hike from the McGurk Meadow trailhead to Stanford Point. A round-trip hike to Dewey Point is 7.8 miles.

TRAILHEAD   The McGurk Meadow trailhead is located 7.5 miles from the start of Glacier Point Road on the left. (Park in the pullout 100 yards up the road.) Follow the trail 1.9 miles to the junction of the Pohono Trail and turn left towards Dewey Point. Note: overnight camping is not allowed to the right of the junction.

TRAIL INFO

RATING Moderate   **HIKING TIME** 4 hours

DISTANCE 10.5 miles, round-trip   **ELEVATION CHANGE** 540 feet

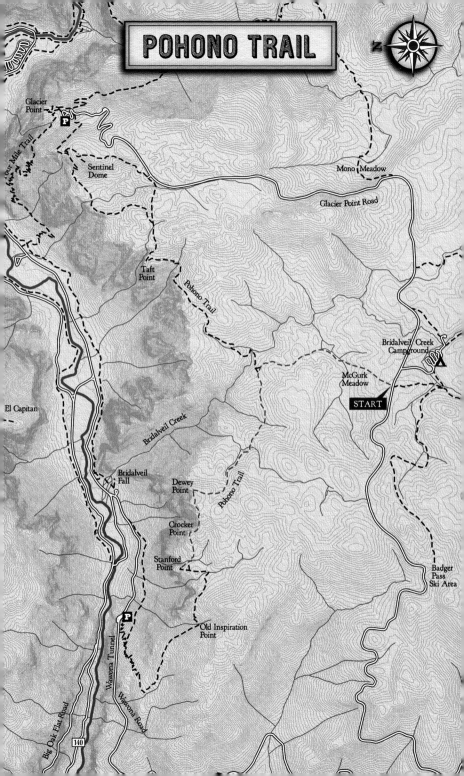

Dewey Point

⚞ THE CLARK RANGE ⚟

SUMMARY For serious backpackers who aren't afraid of multiple days in the wilderness and several thousand feet of elevation change, few hikes in the park are as rewarding as the Clark Range. Seldom visited due to its remote, rugged terrain, the Clark Range features pristine alpine lakes, rocky above-treeline land scapes, and the highest pass in the park: Red Peak Pass (11,200 feet). Highlights along the trail include Ottoway Lakes, Red Peak Pass, and gorgeous Red Devil Lake, where enchanting granite shores offer stunning views of the Clark Range during the day and wide open star gazing at night. To finish off the trip in style reserve a tent cabin at Merced High Sierra Camp and treat yourself to a bed, a hot shower, and a home-cooked meal on your last night. Finish the hike by heading down the Mist Trail to Happy Isles in Yosemite Valley.

TRAILHEAD The hike starts at the Mono Meadows trailhead off Glacier Point Road. Unless you have two cars to shuttle between the start and the finish, leave your car in Yosemite Valley and ride the Glacier Point shuttle to the Mono Meadows trailhead.

TRAIL INFO

RATING Very Strenuous

DISTANCE 46.5 miles

HIKING TIME 6–7 days

ELEVATION CHANGE 7,000 feet

Hiking below Red Peak Pass

Red Devil Lake

Merced Grove

BIG OAK FLAT ROAD

THIS 17-MILE ROAD, which stretches between the park's Big Oak Flat Entrance and Yosemite Valley, offers the most direct route to Yosemite Valley if you're traveling from San Francisco. Although there's little dramatic scenery past the entrance station, the Merced Grove of giant sequoias (below) is worth a visit. Two park campgrounds are also located along Big Oak Flat Road: Crane Flat and Hodgdon Meadow. Both are located far from Yosemite's popular sights, but they might be your best bet for an open campsite if you visit during peak season.

Arguably the most important stop along the road is Crane Flat, located eight miles past the Big Oak Flat Entrance. Named for the sandhill cranes that early explorers found here, Crane Flat was the site of a rowdy saloon in the late 1800s. Back then visiting sheepherders would drown their loneliness in whiskey. Today Crane Flat sells an even more addictive liquid: gasoline. As the only "reasonably" priced gas station anywhere near Yosemite Valley, Crane Flat is one of the most logistically important places in the park, especially if you're about to embark on a long drive up Tioga Road (p.221). The adjacent convenience store also sells cold drinks and snacks.

Southeast of Crane Flat the road descends roughly 12 miles towards Yosemite Valley. As you approach Yosemite Valley, the views grow more and more dramatic. The final descent into the Merced River Canyon offers fabulous glimpses of Half Dome, El Capitan and Bridalveil Fall, and there are a handful of scenic pullouts on the side of the road. At the end of the descent Big Oak Flat Road intersects with Highway 140, which heads to Yosemite Valley.

Merced Grove

Home to about two dozen giant sequoias (p.72), the Merced Grove is often the least crowded of Yosemite's three sequoia groves. The big trees are reached via a 1.5-mile trail, which descends nearly 600 feet from the parking area. The steep hike can be strenuous. Plan on at least two to three hours for a visit, and bring plenty of water—there's no water available at the grove. The Merced Grove parking area is located about 14 miles from Yosemite Valley (30-minute drive) and 5.5 miles from the Big Oak Flat Entrance (10-minute drive).

TIOGA ROAD

★ ★ ★ ★ ★

Clouds Rest from Olmstead Point

TIOGA ROAD

THIS 46-MILE ROAD twists deep into the heart of Yosemite, climbing 3,750 feet to the Sierra's crest and showcasing some of the park's finest alpine scenery. After you've gotten your fill of Yosemite Valley and Glacier Point, Tioga Road should be next on your list. Highlights include Olmstead Point, which showcases bold views of Clouds Rest and Half Dome, and Tenaya Lake, where icy waters reflect massive granite domes. Past Tenaya Lake, Tioga Road skirts Tuolumne Meadows (p.247), then climbs to Tioga Pass—at 9,941 feet, the highest paved road in California. The road then exits the park and plunges over 3,000 feet to the eastern deserts at the base of the Sierra Nevada.

In winter Tioga Road is closed due to heavy snow. When the first snowfall hits (generally by mid-November) Tioga Road shuts down. Its reopening date in the spring depends entirely upon winter snowfall. In 1998 the road was closed until July 1 (a record), but generally Tioga Road opens around mid-May.

Tioga Road begins its ascent at Crane Flat, 16 miles northwest of Yosemite Valley along Big Oak Flat Road (Highway 120). There's a gas station and minimart at Crane Flat. If your tank is running low, it's a good idea to fill up there.

Head northwest from Crane Flat along Tioga Road and soon you'll reach the Tuolumne Grove of giant sequoias. (Another grove of giant sequoias, the Merced Grove, is located 3.5 miles northeast of Crane along Big Oak Flat Road; the Merced Grove showcases about 20 large trees, reached via a 2-mile path.) Past the Tuolumne Grove, Tioga Road ascends through a long stretch of forest, passing turnoffs for White Wolf Lodge and several campgrounds. Eventually the forest gives way to open views, which become increasingly dramatic as you climb higher and higher.

Along the way to Tuolumne Meadows, Tioga Road offers access to some of the finest hikes and backpacks in the park, including Clouds Rest, 10 Lakes, and two popular High Sierra Camps (May Lake and Sunrise). You can also walk down to North Dome, which overlooks Yosemite Valley. Although often ignored by first-time visitors, these hikes are among the finest in the park.

Throughout the summer a free shuttle runs between Olmstead Point and Tioga Pass (check the *Yosemite Guide* for seasonal times and dates). There's also the Tuolumne Meadows Tour & Hikers Bus, which makes a daily run between Yosemite Valley and Tuolumne Meadows, stopping at popular Tioga Road viewpoints and trailheads along the way (209-372-1240).

TIOGA ROAD

Hetch Hetchy Reservoir

Grand Canyon of the Tuolumne

Gl
A

Ten Lakes

May Lake

White Wolf

Tioga Road

Tenaya Lake

Porcupine Flat

3

Tuolumne Grove

Yosemite Creek

2

1

Olmstead Point

North Dome

Sunris

Tamarack Flat

Clouds Rest

Big Oak Flat Road

Yosemite Valley

140

Glacier Point Road

1 Tuolumne Grove

This small grove of giant sequoias (p.72) is often overshadowed by the more famous Mariposa Grove in Wawona, but the Tuolumne Grove is definitely worth a visit if you're enchanted by the big trees. The grove is located about a half mile past the Crane Flat junction. A two-mile round-trip path starts from the parking area and drops about 500 feet as it passes by 25 giant sequoias. Among the notables: a tree with a tunnel cut through the trunk (the tunnel was cut in 1878), and a giant tree that rises nearly 300 feet—one of the tallest giant sequoias in the world.

2 Olmstead Point

Olmstead Point is the most dramatic viewpoint along Tioga Road, famous for its unusual look at Half Dome's backside. But even more impressive is the striking profile of Clouds Rest, a billowing 9,926-foot granite mountain that rises 4,500 feet above Tenaya Canyon. During the Ice Age a massive glacier filled Tenaya Canyon as it flowed towards Yosemite Valley. Olmstead Point was also buried under the ice, and the bedrock here was smoothed out and polished by the glacier as it passed over the rocks. When the glacier melted, boulders embedded in the ice settled on the bedrock, and these boulders, called glacial erratics, are still there today. Several fine examples of glacial erratics can be seen along the quarter-mile geology trail that starts at Olmstead Point.

Half Dome from Olmstead Point

Clouds Rest & Half Dome

"Clouds Rest was fairly enveloped in drifting gossamer films, and the Half Dome loomed up in the garish light like a majestic, living creature clad in the same gauzy, wind-woven drapery."

—John Muir

3 Tenaya Lake

Lying at an elevation of 8,149 feet, this stunning alpine lake is a great place to take a break and bask in the glorious scenery. Several picnic areas are located alongside the road, and an easy two-mile trail skirts the lake's southeastern shore. You can pick up the trail from the sandy beach at the northeastern end of the lake. The natural beach, a popular destination on hot summer days, is the result of freeze-thaw cycles in the winter. When the lake freezes, cracks form in the ice that often fill with water on warm days. When temperatures once again drop below freezing, the water in the cracks freezes and expands, pushing the previously formed ice out towards the shore. As the ice pushes outward, sediment on the bottom of the lake is pushed towards the shore, forming the sandy beach.

Tenaya Lake, like many lakes in the Sierra Nevada, formed when a massive glacier scooped out a basin in the bedrock. In the depths of the Ice Age, the ice here was over 2,000 feet deep. When the glacier melted, the basin filled with water and formed a lake. Today the southwest end of 180-foot deep Tenaya Lake is still partially dammed by debris left in the glacier's wake.

The Ahwahneechee Indians called Tenaya Lake *Pywiack*, "Lake of Shining Rocks." The name Tenaya was given by the Mariposa Battalion, a local militia organized by whites to remove Indians from the mountains. On May 22, 1851 the Battalion captured several dozen Ahwahneechee hiding near the shores of Pywiack. After marching the Indians out of the mountains, Battalion members named the lake Tenaya after the chief of the Ahwahneechee tribe.

Our camp at Lake Tenaya was especially memorable. After supper and some talk by the fire, LeConte and I sauntered through the pine groves to the shore and sat down on a big rock that stands out a little way in the water. The full moon and the stars filled the lake with light ... a slight breeze ruffled the surface, giving rise to ever-changing pictures of wondrous brightness. At first we talked freely, admiring the silvery masses and ripples of light, and the mystic, wavering dance of the stars and rocks and shadows reflected in the unstable mirror. But soon came perfect stillness, earth and sky were inseparably blended and spiritualized, and we could only gaze on the celestial vision in devout, silent, wondering admiration.

—John Muir

∽ NORTH DOME ⌒

SUMMARY   Most hikes to the rim of Yosemite Valley start in the Valley and require several thousand feet of hiking up. But North Dome is reached via a one-way, 4.5-mile trail that heads 600 feet *down* from Tioga Road. You'll still have to hike 600 feet up on the return (with a few extra ups and downs thrown in for good measure), but the effort is worth it. Perched high on top of 7,542-foot North Dome, you'll be treated to sweeping views of Yosemite Valley. To your left, Half Dome's terrifyingly sheer 2,000-foot northwest face looms above. Although normally done as a day hike, North Dome also makes a great backpack. The forested recess behind North Dome has several great campsites, and sunsets here are among the most spectacular in the park. Backpacking note: there is no water near North Dome. Plan on filling up at one of the several streams you'll encounter early on in the hike.

TRAILHEAD   North Dome's trailhead is located at Porcupine Creek (25 miles east of Crane Flat; 15 miles west of Tuolumne Meadows).

TRAIL INFO

RATING Moderate

DISTANCE 9 miles, round-trip

HIKING TIME 4–5 hours

ELEVATION CHANGE 600 feet

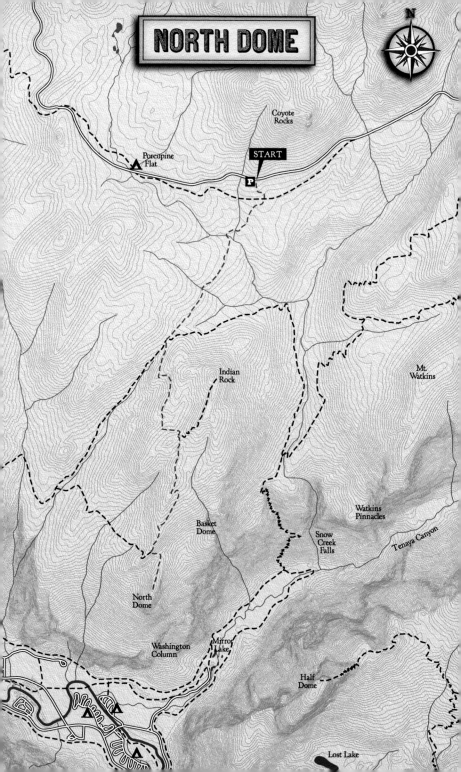

Half Dome

Granite Domes

North Dome (right) and Half Dome (left) are classic examples of Yosemite's famous granite domes. The domes formed when previously overlying rocks eroded along concentric cracks, flaking off like layers of an onion. But why are the domes still bare when the surrounding scenery is covered in forest? A phenomenon called "ice creep" is partly responsible for the absence of vegetation. When snow accumulates in the winter, the bottom layers of snow compress into ice. As sunlight warms the snow, water seeps under the ice and lubricates the rock. The snowpack then slides down the granite and scrapes away accumulated soil and vegetation. Although a few cracks in the granite retain enough soil for some plants to grow, most of the dome remains bare.

North Dome

⊸⊷ MAY LAKE H.S.C. ⊶⊸

SUMMARY May Lake is Yosemite's most accessible High Sierra Camp. The trail to May Lake is just 1.2 miles long with only 500 feet of elevation change. But even if you haven't booked a night in one of the comfy tent cabins, this gorgeous alpine lake (elevation: 9,350 feet) still makes a great day hike or overnight backpack. Looming above the lake is 10,850-foot Mount Hoffman, the geographic center of the park. Although there's no official trail to the top, Mt. Hoffman's summit is a popular destination reached by an unofficial 2-mile trail. If you're comfortable hiking off trail and feel like you can handle the strenuous ascent, Mount Hoffman is a classic destination with sweeping 360-degree views. As John Muir once put it when describing how best to spend one's time in Yosemite: "Go straight to Mt. Hoffman ... From the summit nearly all the Yosemite park is displayed like a map."

TRAILHEAD Turn onto May Lake Road (27 miles east of Crane Flat; 20 miles west of Tuolumne Meadows) and follow the road two miles to the trailhead.

TRAIL INFO

RATING Easy

DISTANCE 2.4 miles, round-trip

HIKING TIME 2 hours

ELEVATION CHANGE 500 feet

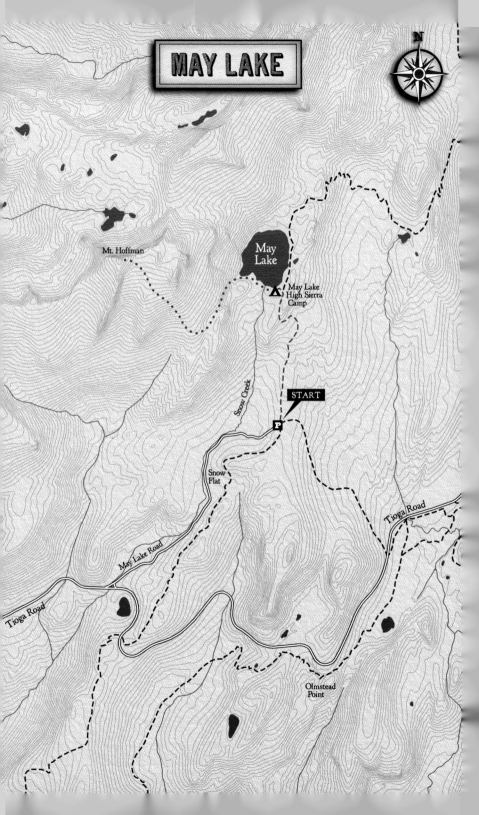

MAY LAKE

N

Mt. Hoffman

May
Lake

May Lake
High Sierra
Camp

Snow Creek

START

P

Snow
Flat

Tioga Road

May Lake Road

Tioga Road

Olmstead
Point

⊰ CLOUDS REST ⊱

SUMMARY Thousands of ambitious hikers set their sights on Half Dome, but savvy Yosemite connoisseurs know that 9,926-foot Clouds Rest offers better views in a shorter distance with mercifully fewer crowds. Nothing against Half Dome—it still offers fantastic views of Yosemite Valley—but Clouds Rest offers great views of the Valley, *plus* amazing views of the High Sierra, plus incredible views 1,000 feet above Half Dome! Simply put: Clouds Rest should be in any serious Yosemite hiker's top five. The trail starts near Tenaya Lake and soon encounters a steep, thousand-foot, switchback-laden ascent. This is the toughest part of the hike (and it sure is nice to get half of the elevation out of the way right at the start). Although Clouds Rest is easily done in a day, there are several good campsites along the way for backpackers.

TRAILHEAD The trail to Clouds Rest starts at the Sunrise Lakes Trailhead at the southwest end of Tenaya Lake. After reaching the top of the steep ascent, the trail splits. Follow the signs to Clouds Rest.

◀ TRAIL INFO ▶

RATING Strenuous

DISTANCE 14.4 miles, round-trip

HIKING TIME 7–8 hours

ELEVATION CHANGE 2,200 feet

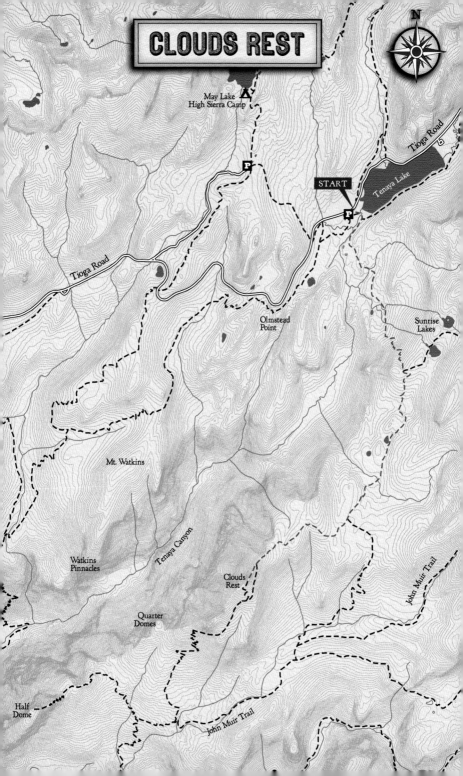

View from Clouds Rest

ᘺ SUNRISE H.S.C. ᘻ

SUMMARY The lush meadow at Sunrise High Sierra Camp offers weary hikers the ultimate in alpine relaxation. Often waterlogged and spongy in the early summer, by mid-summer it's a wildflower-strewn paradise with a serpentine creek flowing through the center. Sparkling views of the surrounding granite peaks leave no doubt why Sunrise was included on the John Muir Trail. But even without the lure of the High Sierra Camp, Sunrise Meadow would still be a popular backpacking destination. Several exceptional campsites are perched on a rise overlooking the meadow, and campers are treated to (drum roll, please!) composting toilets.

TRAILHEAD The most direct route to Sunrise High Sierra Camp (info listed below) starts at the Sunrise Lakes Trailhead at the southwest end of Tenaya Lake. An alternate route starts in Tuolumne Meadows at the Cathedral Lakes Trailhead (p.258) and follows the John Muir Trail down to Sunrise Meadow. Although easier, the Cathedral Lake route is slightly longer (13.2 miles round-trip, 1,300 feet elevation change).

◆ TRAIL INFO ◆

RATING Strenuous	**HIKING TIME** 6–7 hours
DISTANCE 10.4 miles, round-trip	**ELEVATION CHANGE** 1,600 ft.

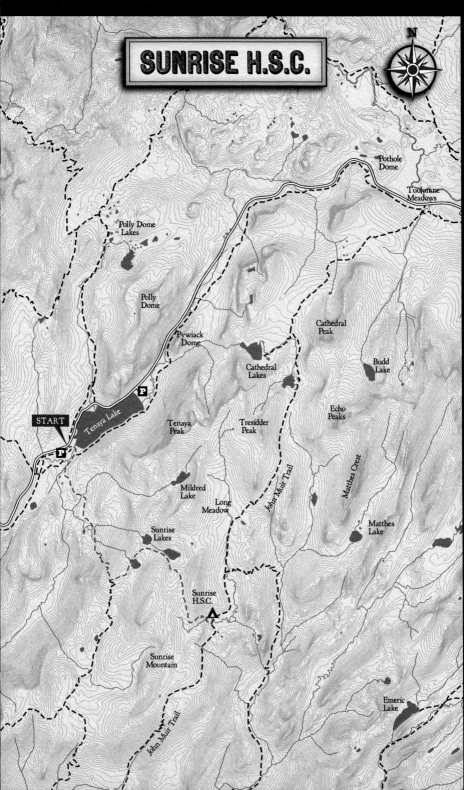

~❧ TEN LAKES ᐒ~

SUMMARY This secluded cluster of lakes is nestled in a granite basin at about 9,000 feet. Despite the name, there are only seven lakes at Ten Lakes (three previously counted bodies of water are now considered ponds). Numerical shortfall aside, Ten Lakes makes a good, long day hike and a superb overnight backpack. There's great fishing, and because the lakes lie below 9,600 feet campfires are allowed at night. The trail to Ten Lakes climbs gradually to Half Moon Meadow, then makes a steep ascent to 9,500-foot Ten Lakes Pass, where you'll be treated to terrific views of the High Sierra, including Mt. Conness and the Sawtooth Ridge. From Ten Lakes Pass descend 500 feet into Ten Lakes Basin. A few hundred yards north of the lakes, the outer rim of Ten Lakes Basin drops thousands of feet into the Grand Canyon of the Tuolumne River (p.284).

TRAILHEAD The hike starts at the Ten Lakes trailhead (20 miles east of Crane Flat; 26 miles west of Tuolumne Meadows). There's a good-sized parking lot across the road from the trailhead.

◀ TRAIL INFO ▶

RATING Strenuous   **HIKING TIME** 6–7 hours

DISTANCE 12.8 miles, round-trip   **ELEVATION CHANGE** 2,000 feet

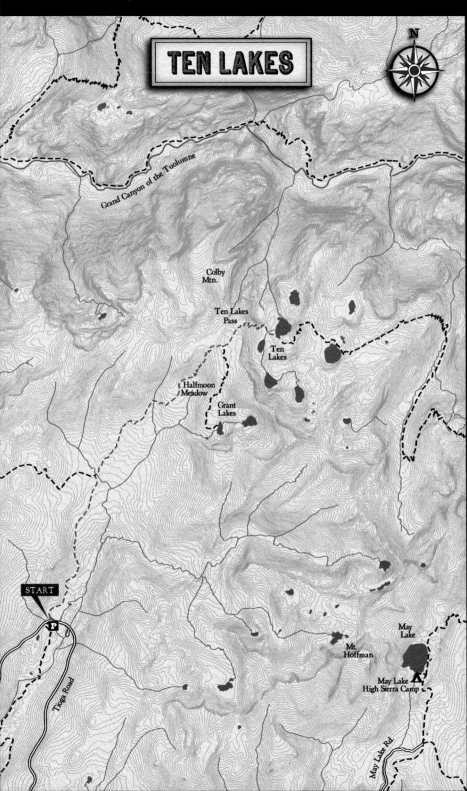

TUOLUMNE
MEADOWS

★ ★ ★ ★ ☆

Tuolumne Meadows & Mount Conness

TUOLUMNE MEADOWS

LYING AT AN elevation of 8,600 feet, Tuolumne Meadows is the gateway to Yosemite's High Sierra—a stunning wilderness of flowery meadows, snow-capped peaks, and miles of sparkling granite. Hiking trails radiate out from Tuolumne (pronounced Too-All-Uh-Me) in all directions, offering hikers and rock climbers access to Yosemite's alpine wonderland. Whether you're looking for an easy stroll, a moderate day hike, or a strenuous week-long backpack, Tuolumne Meadows has it all. Tuolumne is also the Sierra Nevada's largest subalpine meadow, making it a great place to just kick back and relax.

For thousands of years, the Ahwahneechee Indians journeyed from Yosemite Valley to Tuolumne Meadows to trade with the Mono Indians, who lived east of Yosemite. The high elevation also offered the Ahwahneechee relief from Yosemite Valley's summer heat. Fast forward to the present, and not much has changed. In July and August, when Yosemite Valley is plagued with heat spells and crowds, savvy Yosemite visitors head to Tuolumne to cool off high above it all. Temperatures in Tuolumne Meadows are generally 15 to 20 degrees cooler than in Yosemite Valley. While not entirely uncrowded, Tuolumne Meadows never feels like a carnival, and true Sierra solitude is never more than a hike away. (Sweaty hiker note: hot showers can be purchased at Tuolumne Lodge.)

When it comes to Tuolumne hiking, timing is everything. In winter Tuolumne Meadows is often buried under 10–12 feet of snow. Visit in the early spring and many trails might still be covered in snow. Visit just after the snow melts and you'll be fighting off swarms of mosquitoes. Visit after the mosquitoes die down, however, and you'll be treated to High Sierra splendor. Check the park website (nps.gov/yose) for current trail conditions, and ask rangers about mosquitoes before hitting the trail. August and September are consistently good months for hiking in Tuolumne, but September usually brings the first frost. By late September, nights in Tuolumne often dip below freezing.

No matter when you visit Tuolumne, plan on bringing warm clothes. Summer days are famously sunny and warm, but nights can get chilly. Afternoon thundershowers, though infrequent, are possible, and summer snow flurries, though very rare, can occur.

Tuolumne Meadows
BASICS

Getting to Tuolumne Meadows

Located alongside Tioga Road, Tuolumne Meadows is 55 miles (90-minute drive) from Yosemite Valley and 13 miles (30-minute drive) from the town of Lee Vining at the eastern base of the Sierra Nevada. In past years the Tuolumne Meadows Hikers Bus made a daily trip between Yosemite Valley and Tuolumne Meadows from July through mid-September. As this book went to press, the new park concessionaire, Aramark, had not officially announced continuation of this service. For up-to-date info call 209-372-4386 or visit travelyosemite.com. YARTS runs a shuttle between Mammoth Mountain and Yosemite Valley that stops in Tuolumne Meadows. The YARTS shuttle runs daily in July and August and on weekends in June and September (877-989-2787, yarts.com)

Getting Around Tuolumne Meadows

Throughout the summer a free shuttle runs between Olmstead Point and Tioga Pass (check the *Yosemite Guide* for seasonal hours and dates).

Services

TUOLUMNE MEADOWS VISITOR CENTER

This small visitor center is a great place to get up-to-date Tuolumne info: trail conditions, shuttle schedules, weather reports, etc. There are also natural history exhibits and a small bookstore. Open through late September. (209-372-0263)

WILDERNESS CENTER

Pick up wilderness permits at this small building, located a half mile east of Tuolumne Campground, just off Tioga Road. (209-372-8427)

TUOLUMNE STORE

This seasonal store offers a surprisingly good selection of groceries, beer, wine, books and basic camping supplies. Located just west of Tuolumne Campground.

TUOLUMNE MOUNTAIN SHOP

This small store sells an ample selection of outdoor gear—everything from tents to climbing shoes. Located just west of the Tuolumne Store on Tioga Road.

Activities

RANGER PROGRAMS

Free ranger-led walks, hikes and campfire programs are offered throughout the summer and into the fall. Check the *Yosemite Guide* for seasonal dates and times.

YOSEMITE MOUNTAINEERING SCHOOL

Like its counterpart in Yosemite Valley, the Yosemite Mountaineering School in Tuolumne Meadows offers rock climbing lessons for all abilities. (209-372-8435)

TUOLUMNE MEADOWS STABLES

The Tuolumne Meadows Stables offers mule and horseback rides along several nearby trails. Options include 2-hour rides, 4-hour rides, half-day rides, full-day rides and multi-day pack trips. (209-372-8427)

Dining

★ TIOGA PASS RESORT $$ (Brk, Lnch, Din)

More than a wayside restaurant, the Tioga Pass Resort is a High Sierra institution, luring visitors with its great menu and a cozy atmosphere. The food is high on quality, low on pretension, and full of 9,000-foot alpine charm. Located two miles east of Tioga Pass.

★ TUOLUMNE MEADOWS LODGE $$ (Brk, Din)

Tuolumne Lodge offers the only sit down dining experience in Tuolumne Meadows. Diners are seated in random groups at large tables, which means you'll get to know your neighbors. Located next to the front office at Tuolumne Lodge. Reservations required for dinner. Box lunches available if ordered the night before. (209-372-8413)

WHOA NELI DELI $$ (Brk, Lnch, Din)

Located in a Mobil gas station—yes, a Mobil gas station—this otherwise nondescript mini-mart serves shockingly good food. From pizzas and sandwiches to buffalo meatloaf and fish tacos with mango salsa, their menu is extensive and eclectic. Located near the junction of Tioga Road and Highway 395 in Lee Vining. (760-647-1088)

TUOLUMNE MEADOWS GRILL $ (Lnch, Din)

This take-out grill serves cheap, greasy staples like burgers, hot dogs and chicken sandwiches. There are also a handful of healthy options. It ain't gourmet, but it sure tastes good after several days in the backcountry. Located next to the Tuolumne Store.

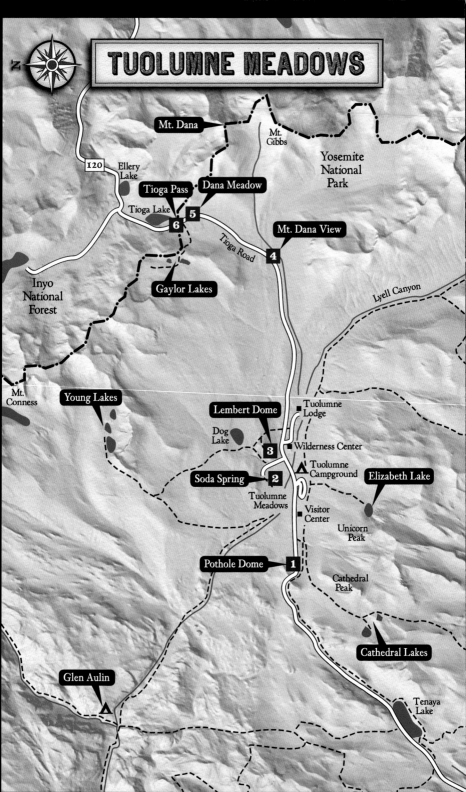

1 Pothole Dome

A 200-foot scramble to the top of this small dome offers great views of Tuolumne Meadows. Pothole Dome is named for a series of rounded depressions ("potholes") on its southern flank. The smooth rock on the southern flank is often mistaken for glacial polish—a glassy veneer created when the underside of a moving glacier buffs the bedrock to a shine—but the polish on Pothole Dome's southern flank was created by water, not ice. During the last Ice Age, water flowed *under* a glacier that covered Pothole Dome. The gritty water, channeled by a tunnel in the ice, flowed uphill over the dome, sculpting the potholes and polishing the rock. Actual glacial polish can be seen on Pothole Dome's eastern slope.

2 Soda Spring/Parsons Lodge

This bubbling, naturally carbonated spring is hardly picturesque, but the views of Tuolumne Meadows and the surrounding peaks make it a great destination. The path to Soda Springs is an easy 1.5 mile stroll—perfect for visitors of all ages. From the Lembert Dome parking area, follow the dirt road north and continue past the metal gate. After checking out Soda Spring, head over to Parsons Lodge (above), a quaint stone lodge built by the Sierra Club in 1914. For decades the building was used as a Sierra Club meeting house. Today Parsons Lodge houses a number of interesting exhibits, and free lectures are offered on summer weekends.

3 Lembert Dome

Looming 900 feet over the eastern end of Tuolumne Meadows, Lembert Dome is named for John-Baptiste Lembert, a sheepherder who homesteaded in Tuolumne Meadows in the late 1800s. In a strange twist of fate, the geological term used to describe formations like Lembert Dome is *roche moutonnée* ("stone sheep"). Roche moutonnées form when glaciers flow over a large rock outcrop, smoothing out a gradual uphill slope. As the glacier overrides the top, it plucks away at the rock below, forming a steep drop-off. A short trail heads to the top of Lembert Dome, which offers stunning 360-degree views of Tuolumne Meadows and the surrounding peaks (p.256).

4 Mt. Dana/Mt. Gibbs View

This roadside pullout along the Dana Fork of the Tuolumne River offers great views of Mt. Dana (on the left) and Mt. Gibbs. The pullout is marked by a small post labeled T36. At 13,053 feet Mt. Dana is the second highest peak in the park. Only Mt. Lyell (13,114 feet) is taller. Mt. Gibbs (12,764 feet) is the fifth highest peak in the park. While savoring the view of Mt. Dana and Mt. Gibbs, notice their dark coloration. The two peaks are composed of ancient metamorphic rocks that once covered all of Yosemite's granite. This is one of the few places in the park where these ancient metamorphic rocks are still visible. A strenuous 3-mile hike heads to the top of Mt. Dana (p.276).

5 Dana Meadow

This beautiful meadow, located just west of the park boundary, lies 1,000 feet higher than Tuolumne Meadows. Twenty thousand years ago both meadows were buried under a massive glacier, but when global temperatures warmed around 15,000 years ago the ice started to melt. As the glacier retreated, huge chunks of ice broke off and formed depressions in the ground called *kettles*, which ultimately filled with water. The small ponds you see today are remnants of those kettles. You may also notice dozens of fallen trees on the north side of the meadow. These trees were knocked down several decades ago when an avalanche raced down the slopes above the meadow, which explains why all of the fallen trees point downhill.

6 Tioga Pass

At 9,941 feet, Tioga Pass (above) is the highest highway pass in California. It marks Yosemite's eastern boundary, which is also the watershed boundary for the Tuolumne River. (Precipitation that falls west of Tioga Pass flows down the Tuolumne River and is destined for San Francisco; precipitation that falls east of Tioga Pass flows down Lee Vining Creek towards the Great Basin Desert.) As Highway 120 heads east from Tioga Pass, it plunges down the sheer eastern slope of the Sierra Nevada to the small town of Lee Vining. Along the way you'll be treated to great views of Tioga Lake, Ellery Lake and Lee Vining Canyon.

East of Tioga Pass, Tioga Road enters one of its most dramatic stretches. It starts innocently enough, twisting through pine forests and passing a pair of beautiful alpine lakes. Then, suddenly, Tioga Road makes a sharp turn north. Spread out below is Lee Vining Canyon, a startling expanse that slices through the crest of the Sierra Nevada and extends to the town of Lee Vining, which lies at the eastern base of the mountains. Over the next nine miles, Tioga Road clings to the steep mountainside as it plummets over 2,000 feet. Not to worry. Whatever you lose in brake pads you'll gain in majestic scenery. (Tip: shift into low gear during the descent.) And if you think the drive is tough, try running up the road. That's what over 100 masochists do each September during the Tioga Pass Run. This 12.4-mile race, which starts in Lee Vining and ends at Tioga Pass, climbs 3,200 feet. The 2015 winner, Patrick Parsel, completed the race in under 90 minutes.

ᔔ LEMBERT DOME ᖚ

SUMMARY   For a relatively quick Tuolumne hike with dramatic views, nothing beats Lembert Dome. Rising 9,450-feet over the east end of Tuolumne Meadows, Lembert Dome offers panoramic views of the High Sierra, including peaks along the eastern crest of the Sierra and the Cathedral Range. From the Dog Lake parking area the trail climbs through a forest, heads west at a junction, and emerges onto an open stretch of bare granite. At this point there's no official trail, but a series of cairns (small rock piles) will guide you towards the summit. With broad views of the western horizon, Lembert Dome is a fantastic spot to watch the sunset (make sure to bring a flashlight or headlight for the hike down).

TRAILHEAD   The best (and shortest) route to the top of Lembert Dome starts from the Dog Lake parking area near Tuolumne Lodge. Take the free shuttle, or drive east on Tioga Road from Tuolumne Meadows and turn right towards Tuolumne Lodge. Follow the road to the Dog Lake parking area. The trail starts at the upper end of the parking area and crosses Tioga Road.

TRAIL INFO

RATING Moderate   **HIKING TIME** 1 hour

DISTANCE 1.6 miles, round-trip   **ELEVATION CHANGE** 850 feet

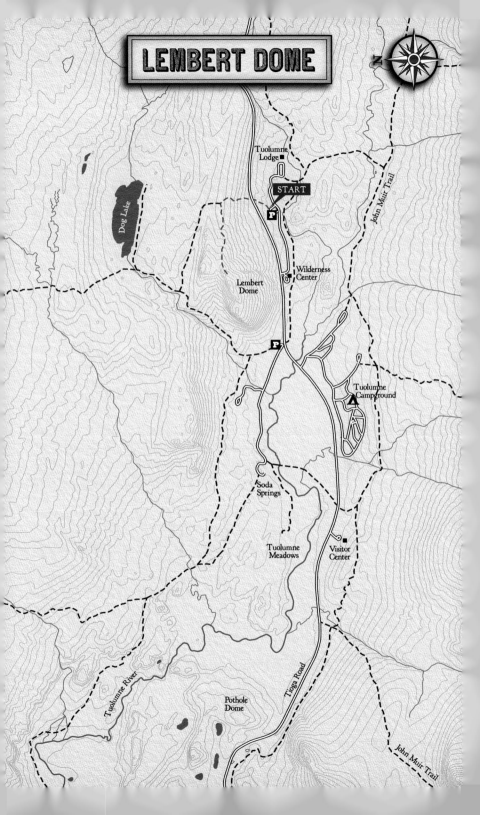

⇜ CATHEDRAL LAKES ⇝

SUMMARY   These two small lakes, nestled along the John Muir Trail, are among the prettiest in Yosemite. Kick back on the smooth granite shores of Lower Cathedral Lake and soak in the dramatic views of Cathedral Peak, or continue to the flower-strewn meadows surrounding Upper Cathedral Lake and check out the peak from a different perspective. The hike to Cathedral Lakes is an uphill workout, but the scenery is definitely worth it. Lower Cathedral Lake, reached via a half-mile spur trail, is the larger of the two. If you've got a limited amount of time or energy, spend it there. But if your inner alpine lake lover is thirsting for more, continue a half mile past the spur trail to Upper Cathedral Lake. Backpacking note: Upper Cathedral Lake is a popular camping spot, but overnight camping is not allowed at Lower Cathedral Lake.

TRAILHEAD   The trail to Cathedral Lakes starts about 1.5 miles west of the Tuolumne Visitor Center. Parking is often tight due to the trail's popularity, so consider riding the free shuttle from the Visitors Center.

TRAIL INFO

RATING Moderate

HIKING TIME 4–6 hours

DISTANCE 7.5 miles, round-trip

ELEVATION CHANGE 1,000 feet

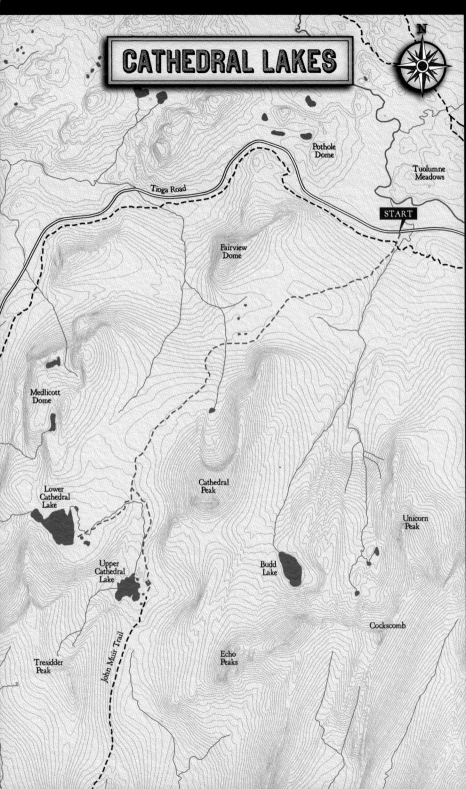

~ ELIZABETH LAKE ~

SUMMARY   While not as dramatic as Cathedral Lakes, Elizabeth Lake is a close runner-up, with lush meadows and shimmering reflections of the granite peaks above. The round-trip hike is also three miles shorter—perfect for lake lovers with a limited amount of time. Once at Elizabeth Lake, check out Unicorn Peak towering above. The peak's "peculiar horn-shaped outline"—though hardly unicorn-esque from this angle—inspired the Whitney Survey to name it after the mythical creature. Experienced hikers can attempt a rugged scramble to the top of Unicorn Peak, which offers terrific 10,900-foot views of Tuolumne Meadows, but most visitors will be content to simply lounge around the lake. Following snowy winters, a long snow chute often lingers at the far end of the lake. Note: camping is not allowed at Elizabeth Lake.

TRAILHEAD   The trail to Elizabeth Lake starts in the Tuolumne Campground near the group camp restrooms on the B Loop. Signs in the campground will direct you to the trailhead. Don't be put off by the initial steep climb—the trail soon mellows out.

TRAIL INFO

RATING Moderate	**HIKING TIME** 3–4 hours
DISTANCE 4.6 miles, round-trip	**ELEVATION CHANGE** 850 feet

ᘒ GLEN AULIN H.S.C. ᕗ

SUMMARY Situated next to one of Yosemite's most spectacular backcountry waterfalls, Glen Aulin is many people's favorite High Sierra Camp. Even better: the hike to Glen Aulin from Tuolumne Meadows is almost entirely downhill, following the cascading Tuolumne River. You'll still have to hike uphill on the way back, but after a good night's rest in a comfy tent cabin you'll be ready to hit the trail. Glen Aulin is also the jumping off point for several long backpacks, including the Grand Canyon of the Tuolumne (p.284) and Matterhorn Canyon (p.288). Due to Glen Aulin's popularity, a backpackers' campground with bear boxes and toilets is located behind the High Sierra Camp. (To protect the water quality of the Tuolumne drainage, which ends up in San Francisco's water supply, Glen Aulin's high-tech composting toilet was built at a cost of several hundred thousand dollars—provoking some in the press to call it the "two-seat wonder.")

TRAILHEAD From the Lembert Dome parking area, follow the broad path towards Soda Springs and then follow the signs to Glen Aulin.

TRAIL INFO

RATING Moderate	**HIKING TIME** 6–8 hours
DISTANCE 10.4 miles, round-trip	**ELEVATION CHANGE** 800 feet

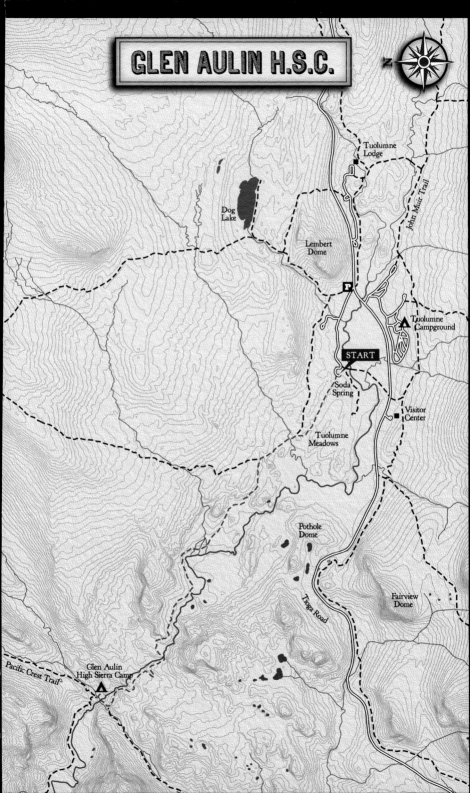

⇥ GAYLOR LAKES ⇤

SUMMARY This dramatic hike brings you to two shimmering lakes near the ruins of an old mining camp. Starting at an elevation of 10,000 feet, it's one of the highest day hikes in Yosemite—which means open scenery with terrific views of the surrounding High Sierra. The trail starts near the park's eastern boundary and immediately climbs a steep ridge with great views of Dana Meadow. From there the trail descends to the first lake, skirting the northern shore as the jagged peaks of the Cathedral Range seem to rise above the water to the west. Continue to the upper lake and you'll find permanent snowfields lying in the shade of the mountains. After wrapping around the shore, the trail climbs a small ridge that provides sweeping views of both lakes. Nearby are the crumbling remains of the Great Sierra Mine, a failed silver-mining operation that was established here in the 1800s. Note: camping is not allowed at Gaylor Lakes.

TRAILHEAD The trail starts from the small parking area with a restroom just west of the Tioga Pass entrance station. You can also ride the free shuttle, which makes a handful of stops at Tioga Pass throughout the day during the summer.

TRAIL INFO

RATING Moderate

DISTANCE 5 miles, round-trip

HIKING TIME 2–3 hours

ELEVATION CHANGE 800 feet

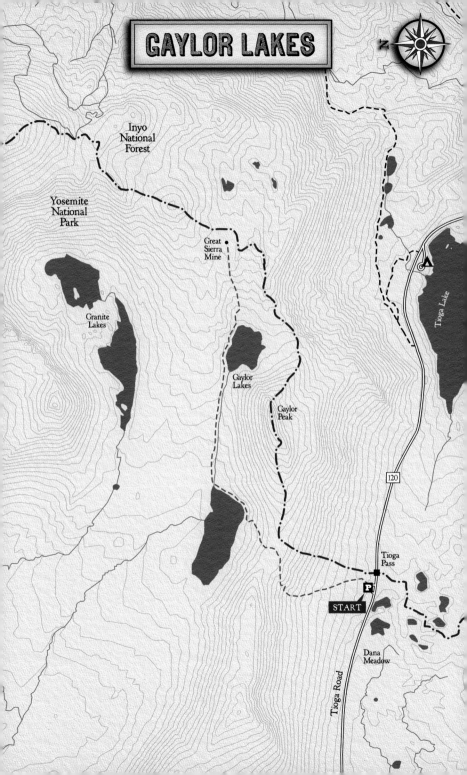

GAYLOR LAKES

N

Inyo National Forest

Yosemite National Park

Great Sierra Mine

Granite Lakes

Gaylor Lakes

Gaylor Peak

Tioga Lake

120

Tioga Pass

START

Dana Meadow

Tioga Road

⋰ᘒ YOUNG LAKES ᘖ⋰

SUMMARY   These three picture-perfect lakes make a long, rewarding day hike or a terrific overnight backpack. Lower Young Lake, surrounded by lodgepole pines and dramatic granite, is distinguished by its sandy beaches. Middle Young Lake is the smallest of the three, and Upper Young Lake, located above treeline, offers the most spectacular scenery. The shortest, most scenic route to Young Lakes heads towards Dog Lake and continues north. (Note: an alternate route, less steep but longer, branches off the Glen Aulin trail about a mile past Soda Springs.) If you're spending at least two nights at Young Lakes, nearby Mt. Conness makes a spectacular day hike—but only for rugged hikers who are used to off-trail travel. To climb Mt. Conness, head north from Middle or Upper Young Lake, skirt the ravine towards a series of marshy ponds, and pick up the unofficial use trail. Backpacking note: campfires are not allowed at Young Lakes.

TRAILHEAD   The trailhead via Dog Lake starts near the picnic tables at the Lembert Dome parking area. The info listed below is for a hike to Lower Young Lake; Upper Young Lake is about 0.7 miles beyond Lower Young Lake.

TRAIL INFO

RATING Strenuous	**HIKING TIME** 8–10 hours
DISTANCE 13.5 miles, round-trip	**ELEVATION CHANGE** 1,500 feet

YOUNG LAKES

Roosevelt
Lake

Conness Lakes

Conness Glacier

Inyo
National
Forest

Mt.
Conness

Alpine
Lake

White
Mountain

Skelton
Lakes

Ragged
Peak

Young Lakes

Dog Lake

START

Lembert
Dome

P

Tuolumne
Meadows

Tioga Road

John Muir Trail

"The mighty Sierra, miles in height ... so gloriously colored and so radiant, it seemed not clothed with light but wholly composed of it, like the wall of some celestial city .... Then it seemed to me that the Sierra should be called, not the Nevada or Snowy Range, but the Range of Light."

—John Muir

Mount Conness (left) from Young Lakes

Hiking between Young Lakes & Mt. Conness

◁ MOUNT CONNESS ▷

SUMMARY   At 12,590 feet Mount Conness is the eighth tallest peak in Yosemite, and the tallest peak in the Sierra Nevada north of Tioga Road. It's sheer southwest face—a favorite among rock climbers—is one of the High Sierra's most iconic sights. The summit of Conness lies on the national park boundary. The most direct route starts outside the park in the adjacent Inyo National Forest. From Sawmill Campground an unofficial trail climbs to Alpine Lake, then ascends to a wide plateau. The final push navigates a narrow knife edge—sure to quicken the pulse of all but the most battle-hardened hikers. The reward: sweeping views of the Sierra Nevada, including Conness Glacier, the second-largest glacier in the park after Lyell Glacier (p.56). Note: an easier but longer route to the top of Conness starts from Young Lakes (p.266).

TRAILHEAD   From Tioga Pass drive 2.1 miles north, then turn left onto Saddlebag Lake Road. Follow the dirt road 1.6 miles to Sawmill Campground. The trail starts from the northwest end of the campground.

TRAIL INFO

RATING: Difficult

HIKING TIME: 6–8 Hours

DISTANCE: 8 miles, round-trip

ELEVATION CHANGE: 2,748 ft.

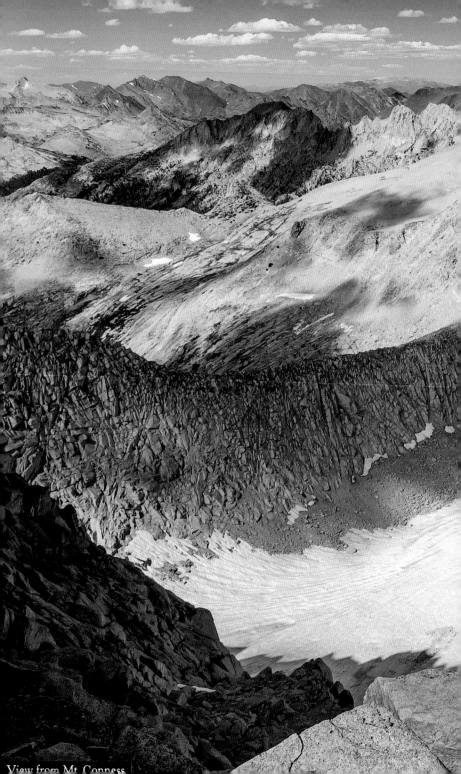

View from Mt. Conness

◄ MOUNT DANA ►

SUMMARY   At 13,053 feet, Mount Dana is the second highest peak in the park after Mount Lyell (13,114 feet). And while Mount Lyell (p.56) requires a rugged, multi-day backpack and technical climbing, Mt. Dana can be done in an afternoon. Perched on the eastern crest of the Sierra Nevada, you'll be treated to 360-degree views of the High Sierra, Mono Lake and the eastern deserts. The unofficial—yet well-worn—trail to the top starts at the Tioga Pass Entrance Station and climbs 1,700 feet to an open ridge. The final 1,000 feet requires a scamper up scree (loose rocks). The final ascent can be confusing. Stay near the eastern edge and look for cairns (small rock piles) to guide you. Note: Mount Dana is often covered in snow well into the summer—ask about conditions before your hike. Note #2: if you see dark clouds approaching, do not attempt this hike—you do not want to be this high up during one of the Sierra Nevada's legendary thunderstorms.

TRAILHEAD   The trail to Mount Dana starts from the small parking area adjacent to the Tioga Pass Entrance Station. Ask the ranger at the kiosk for directions to the top, then follow the well-worn path east.

TRAIL INFO

RATING Very Strenuous	**HIKING TIME** 5–6 hours
DISTANCE 5.8 miles, round-trip	**ELEVATION CHANGE** 3,100 feet

View from Mt. Dana

Mono Lake

This alkaline lake, lying in the desert just east of Yosemite, is famous for tufa towers: unusual calcium carbonate spires, formed at underwater springs, that have recently been exposed due to low lake levels.

In 1941 the city of Los Angeles extended its aqueduct system to divert water flowing into Mono Lake. The lake lost one-third of its surface area, and Negit Island, which previously lay in the center of the lake, turned into a peninsula. The island had been a critical nesting site for birds. Over 50,000 gulls, 85% of California's breeding population, nest at Mono Lake, and when the island became a peninsula coyotes marched across to feast on bird eggs. In 1978 the Mono Lake Committee teamed up with the Audubon Society to restore Mono Lake. In 1994 the lake's tributary streams won legal protection, and the lake's levels have been slowly rising since. Today the lake covers roughly 70 square miles—about twice the size of San Francisco.

In the depths of the ice age 20,000 years ago, Mono Lake was much larger. The surface of that ancient lake, called Lake Russell, lay at an elevation of 7,140 feet—nearly 750 feet higher than today. Glaciers descending from the

eastern Sierra Nevada emptied directly into the lake, calving off icebergs into the water. As temperatures warmed, Mono Lake shrunk. Because the lake has no outlet, dissolved salts from runoff concentrated over time. Today nearly 300 million tons of salt are dissolved in Mono Lake, making it 2.5 times saltier than the ocean.

Mono Lake is too salty for fish, but roughly five *trillion* brine shrimp inhabit the waters in the warm, summer months. The shrimp are an important food source for the roughly two million migratory birds that visit Mono Lake each year. The lake is also home to strange "scuba diving" alkali flies. Most flies avoid water so as not to drown or be eaten by fish. But in fish-free Mono Lake, the underwater world offers tasty algae and protection from predators. Alkali flies here evolved unusually hairy, waxy bodies that trap air bubbles, allowing them to stay underwater for up to 15 minutes.

Mono Lake was named after the Mono Indians, who gathered alkali fly larvae along its shore. They considered crushed fly larvae a delicacy. As one white explorer noted in 1863, "The Indians gave me some; it does not taste bad, and if one were ignorant of its origin, it would make fine soup."

Mono Lake from Mt. Dana

⚜ VOGELSANG H.S.C. ⚜

SUMMARY   At 10,100 feet, Vogelsang is the highest High Sierra Camp. While the other four High Sierra Camps are nestled among stately forests, Vogelsang is located above treeline, providing terrific views of the surrounding peaks. If you find yourself enthralled by Yosemite's granite landscapes, this is definitely the High Sierra Camp for you. In addition to grand views, there's a gurgling creek flowing through lush meadows—a great place to bask in the Sierra sunshine. Five hundred feet above the High Sierra Camp is gorgeous Vogelsang Lake, nestled in a granite bowl between Vogelsang Peak (11,516) and Fletcher Peak (11,410). Backpackers heading to Vogelsang should seriously consider the 19-mile loop that passes Evelyn Lake and heads back to the trailhead via Lyell Canyon—one of the finest three-day backpacks in the park.

TRAILHEAD   The trail to Vogelsang starts from the parking area at Tuolumne Lodge. The lodge parking area is for guests only, so park in the nearby Dog Lake parking area or ride the free shuttle. Follow the John Muir Trail about a mile to Rafferty Creek, then head towards Vogelsang.

TRAIL INFO

RATING Strenuous	**HIKING TIME** 7–8 hours
DISTANCE 13.6 miles, round-trip	**ELEVATION CHANGE** 1,500 feet

✑ GRAND CANYON ᵒᶠₜₕₑTUOLUMNE ᔐ

SUMMARY   This rugged backpack descends 4,700 feet down the stunning Grand Canyon of the Tuolumne River, then climbs 3,600 feet up to White Wolf Lodge. It's one of the most physically demanding backpacks in the park, but it's worth it. In places, the Grand Canyon of the Tuolumne River rivals Arizona's Grand Canyon in depth, and as you descend you'll be treated to dozens of roaring cascades. The most famous is Waterwheel Falls, where the river glides down a smooth granite slope, then explodes into a series of huge rooster-tail arcs. The trail continues below 5,000 feet in elevation, where black oaks and chaparral are common. (Watch out for rattlesnakes.) Spend the night in Pate Valley and rest up for the next day's grueling ascent. After reaching White Wolf, you'll be ready for a hot shower and a cozy bed. Book a night at White Wolf Lodge before your trip and finish off the hike in style.

TRAILHEAD   Hike down to Glen Aulin (p.262) from Tuolumne Meadows. From Glen Aulin continue following the Tuolumne River downhill.

TRAIL INFO

RATING Very Strenuous   **HIKING TIME** 2–3 days

DISTANCE 28 miles, one-way   **ELEVATION CHANGE** 4,700 feet

GRAND CANYON OF THE TUOLUMNE

Tuolumne
Meadows

START

Glen Aulin
High Sierra Camp

Sunrise
High Sierra Camp

Tenaya
Lake

Waterwheel
Falls

May Lake
High Sierra Camp

Ten Lakes

Muir
Gorge

Porcupine
Flat

Tioga Road

Pate
Valley

Yosemite
Creek

White
Wolf

Hetch Hetchy
Reservoir

"For miles the river is one wild, exulting, on-rushing mass ... gliding in magnificent silver plumes, dashing and foaming through huge boulder-dams, leaping high into the air in wheel-like whirls ... singing in exuberance of mountain energy."

—John Muir

Waterwheel Falls

⌐∂ MATTERHORN CANYON ᖙ⌐

SUMMARY   Lying in the remote northeast corner of the park, Matterhorn Canyon is one of the most spectacular and seldom visited locations in Yosemite. Getting here requires several days of backpacking through rugged wilderness, but for quintessential High Sierra beauty—snow-capped granite peaks, flowery meadows, glacially carved U-shaped valleys—few hikes in the Sierra Nevada can compare. After following the Pacific Crest Trail for 20 miles from Tuolumne Meadows, you'll head north into Matterhorn Canyon. The jagged Sawtooth Range looms above as you march up to Burro Pass (10,600 feet). After savoring the dramatic views, drop down into the meadowy, boulder-strewn canyon that heads to Mule Pass (10,400 feet). Say goodbye to Yosemite as you enter the Hoover Wilderness, which treats you to a handful of idyllic lakes before the hike ends at bustling, touristy Twin Lakes.

TRAILHEAD   From Tuolumne Meadows head to Glen Aulin (p.262), then follow the Pacific Crest Trail through Cold Canyon. Note: this one-way trip ends at Twin Lakes, where you can leave your car for several days for a small fee.

TRAIL INFO

RATING Very Strenuous   **HIKING TIME** 6–8 days

DISTANCE 38.4 miles, round-trip   **ELEVATION CHANGE** 3,500 feet

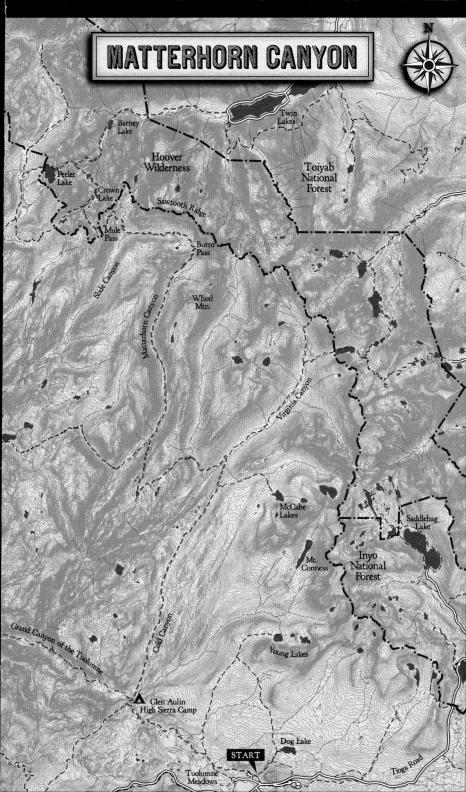

Matterhorn Canyon

U–Shaped Valleys

Matterhorn Canyon and the surrounding High Sierra offer some of the best examples of U-shaped valleys in Yosemite. Prior to the Ice Age, the Sierra Nevada was filled with steep, V-shaped valleys cut by tumbling streams over millions of years. During the depths of the Ice Age, massive glaciers flowed through the V-shaped valleys, gouging out their sides and leaving graceful, U-shaped valleys in their wake. But the highest peaks (including the Sawtooth Range, pictured above) remained above the flowing ice and maintained their jagged profiles.

WAWONA

LOCATED AT THE southernmost tip of Yosemite, Wawona is unremarkable compared to the rest of the park. There's little in the way of dramatic scenery—no sheer cliffs or thousand-foot waterfalls, just a lazy meadow rolling through the forest. Still, Wawona is noteworthy for three things: the Mariposa Grove of giant sequoias, the Big Trees Lodge (formerly Wawona Hotel, see page 36) and the Pioneer History Center.

The Mariposa Grove, located just east of the park's South Entrance Station, is justly famous as the largest grove of giant sequoias in the park. Among its 500+ specimens is Grizzly Giant, the largest tree in the park. About six miles northwest of the Mariposa Grove you'll find Big Trees Lodge and the Pioneer History Center. Adjacent to the Hotel is the Wawona Information Center (209-375-9531), a small building where knowledgeable staff answer questions, issue wilderness permits, and sell books and maps. Just north of the hotel is the Wawona Store, which sells groceries and other basics. A post office and gas station (24-hour credit card payment accepted) are also located nearby. There's no gas in Yosemite Valley—25 miles distant—so if you're heading that way it's a good idea to fill up in Wawona. One mile northwest of the gas station is Wawona Campground, where free ranger-led campfire programs are often held at night. Nature walks and other programs are also offered (check the *Yosemite Guide* for times and dates).

For hundreds of years, native tribes lived near present-day Wawona along the banks of the South Fork of the Merced River. They called the area as *Pallachun* ("Good Place to Stop"). In the fall, when the river ran low, the Indians dumped large quantities of crushed soaproot into the water. According to Galen Clark (p.98), who moved to the area in 1856, the soaproot "roiled the water and made it somewhat foamy. The fish were soon affected by it, became stupid with a sort of strangulation, and rose to the surface, where they were easily captured by the Indians with their scoop baskets."

Shortly after moving here, Clark opened a small hotel catering to tourists on their way to Yosemite Valley. It was said that of all the supplies delivered to Clark's Station, cases of wine, whiskey and brandy far outnumbered cases of food. Clark was a popular host, but a lousy businessman, and in 1874 he sold his hotel to the Washburn brothers. In 1879 they built the current hotel, and in 1882 they renamed the area "Wawona"—the supposed Indian name for giant sequoias. It's claimed the word is an imitation of a hooting owl, which is considered the guardian spirit of the Big Trees.

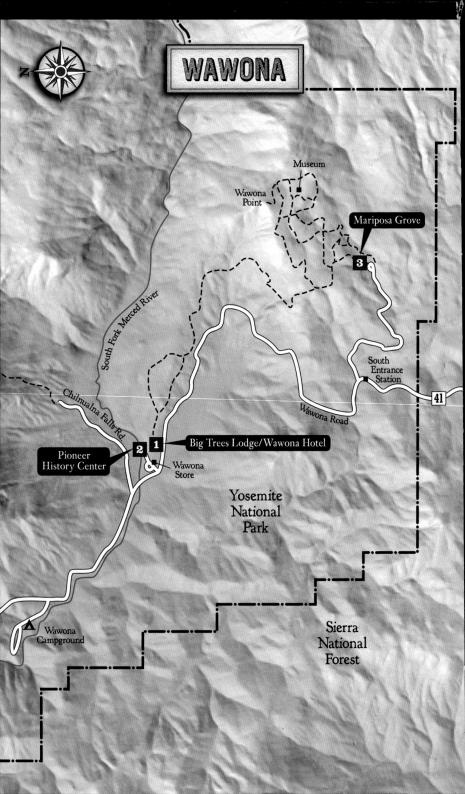

1 Big Trees Lodge (Wawona Hotel)

This beautiful hotel, built in 1879 as the Wawona Hotel (see page 36), is full of Victorian charm. In 1888 a popular guidebook depicted the Wawona Hotel with a dramatic fountain in front, despite the fact that no fountain existed. So many guests complained about the missing fountain that the owners installed one—and it continues to greet visitors to this day. Even if you're not a guest, the elegant dining room serves delicious food (209-375-1425), and local celebrity Tom Bopp frequently plays piano in the lobby/lounge. Saturday BBQs on the lawn are another summer treat, as well as evening cocktails on the front porch. The hotel's Golf Shop (209-375-6572) offers rentals and organizes tee times on the nine-hole golf course in front of the hotel.

2 Pioneer History Center

This small cluster of historic buildings (relocated here in the 1960s from other parts of the park) lies just beyond the Wawona Store. There are cabins, a jail, a Wells Fargo office, a blacksmith shop, a collection of vintage stagecoaches and (for those who prefer the real thing) horse-drawn stage rides. The ten-minute ride costs a few dollars per person. Walk across the covered bridge—one of only a half dozen in California—to the main square and look for posted signs listing dates and times for stage rides and other activities, including campfires and weekend barn dances.

Grizzly Giant

3 Mariposa Grove

Mariposa Grove features Yosemite's largest collection of giant sequoias (p.72), with nearly 500 massive trees scattered throughout 250 acres. Teddy Roosevelt once compared it to a "great solemn cathedral."

Mariposa Grove's most famous tree, Grizzly Giant, is roughly 1,800 years old. Located about a mile from the entrance, Grizzly Giant is over 200 feet high with a base 30 feet in diameter. Its volume has been estimated at 34,000 cubic feet, and one of its branches is over six feet in diameter—larger than the trunks of most full-grown trees in the park.

Mariposa Grove was first protected by Abraham Lincoln in 1864 as part of the Yosemite Grant (p.99). A few decades later, tunnels were cut into two of the trees, one of which became so weakened that it toppled over in a winter storm. Paved roads were also constructed to aid visitor access, but in places the asphalt was laid directly on top of giant sequoia roots. The roads also disrupted Mariposa Grove's natural water flow. On June 30, 2014, the 150th anniversary of the Yosemite Grant, a plan was announced to remove the asphalt and replace it with hiking trails and elevated wooden walkways. The new trails reduce soil erosion and improve water flow, helping protect these magnificent trees for generations to come.

Start your visit at the Welcome Plaza near Yosemite's South Entrance. From there you can catch a free shuttle to Mariposa Grove's entrance. In winter snowshoers and cross-country skiers can enjoy the trails through the grove.

HETCH HETCHY

LOCATED ROUGHLY 12 miles northeast of the park's Big Oak Flat Entrance—40 miles from Yosemite Valley—Hetch Hetchy is definitely off the beaten path. If you're visiting Yosemite for the first time, spend your time elsewhere. But if you're fascinated by the reservoir's tumultuous history, Hetch Hetchy and its springtime waterfalls are worth a look.

Today Hetch Hetchy is an 8-mile long, 117 billion gallon reservoir. Each day 220 million gallons of Hetch Hetchy water are delivered to 2.4 million consumers in the San Francisco Bay Area. The water, which flows downhill along a 167-mile aqueduct, is so pure that it's usually exempted from federal water filtration requirements. And hydropower from O'Shaughnessy Dam generates 1.7 billion kilowatt-hours annually—enough to power 325,000 Bay Area households.

Before the dam was completed in 1923, Hetch Hetchy was a beautiful valley that was, in many ways, comparable to Yosemite. The first white man to set eyes on Hetch Hetchy was Nathan Screech, who arrived in the 1850s. Screech encountered several Indians cooking a plant called *hatchhatchie*, and the word, later anglicized to "Hetch Hetchy," became the name of the valley.

When San Francisco politicians proposed flooding Hetch Hetchy in the early 1900s, John Muir and the Sierra Club fought back. Teddy Roosevelt twice vetoed legislation to build the dam, but in 1913 Woodrow Wilson signed the Raker Act, which authorized the dam. In 1987 Secretary of the Interior Donald Hodel suggested tearing down the dam and restoring Hetch Hetchy Valley. Hodel's plan was opposed by California Congresswoman Nancy Pelosi and then-Mayor of San Francisco Dianne Feinstein, who called the plan the worst idea to come from the Reagan Administration since the sale of arms to Iran.

In 1999 the nonprofit group Restore Hetch Hetchy was founded, and in 2006 California's Department of Water Resources released a report that found "no fatal flaws in the restoration concept that would preclude additional study." Cost estimates of removing the dam range anywhere from one to ten billion dollars.

Hetch Hetchy is only open during daylight hours. To get there, exit Yosemite via the Big Oak Flat Entrance, drive one mile, and turn right onto Evergreen Road. Continue roughly seven miles to Mather Campground, then turn right towards the Hetch Hetchy Entrance Station. From the entrance it's about eight miles to Hetch Hetchy. There's a parking area next to the dam, and an easy 2.5 mile trail skirts the reservoir's northern shore en route to Tueeulala and Wapama Falls. The trail starts at the large tunnel next to the dam.

Over 150,000 copies sold

Travel tips, ... eskaiser.com